THE NEW ALPHABET   Edited by Bernd Scherer, with contributions by
Ann Cotten, Yuk Hui, Ben Lerner, Bernd Scherer, Kanako Tada, and Wolfgang
Tillmans

The New Alphabet

Edited by
Bernd Scherer

Contents

Bernd Scherer. Introduction — 5

Ben Lerner. ABCs: A Holiday Card for Alexander Kluge — 11

Ann Cotten. イロハ — 15

Ann Cotten. 表語文字 — Gods, Logographs, and Dad-Jokes — 18

Bernd Scherer. Cosmology of Perspectives
and Digital Code — 25

Wolfgang Tillmans. From the project
Neue Welt 2011 – 2020, 2020 — 37

Ann Cotten. Notes on Writing Systems — 48

Ann Cotten and Kanako Tada. Reexploring Kanji
Body System — 52

Yuk Hui. On the Cosmotechnical Nature of Writing — 56

Ben Lerner. From *The Hatred of Poetry* — 72

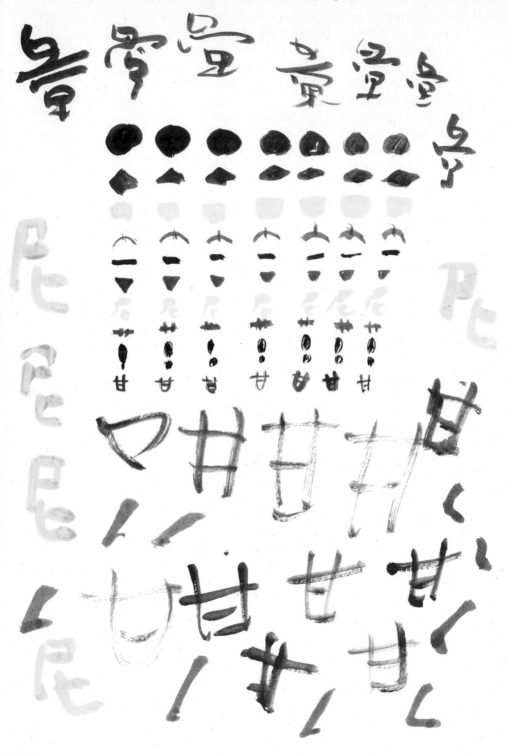

The New Alphabet

"My Robinson has no Bible but Parmenides' poem and the fragments from Heraclitus. I always thought that I too would take
the Bible with me to a desert island, but the idea of the Parmenidean poem, this small dark sun, confronts us with imperturbable being; and in addition, my Heraclitus never ceases
to make reality more complex, to combine opposites and connect
antagonisms in a unity of fire, transforming everything into
a constant becoming: To me, both seem to form an inexhaust-
ible place to keep you occupied during one hundred years of
solitude."[1]

In these "notes from the workshop," Patrick Chamoiseau refers to
two basic positions—the positions of Parmenides and Heraclitus—
that are fundamental to his novel *L'Empreinte à Crusoé* (Crusoe's
Footprint). For the Martinique-born author, the figure of Robinson
Crusoe reflects the challenge of the Caribbean as a laboratory of
modernity. The challenge is to start from scratch and reinvent your-
self. Such is the Parmenidean experience of being confronted with
"imperturbable being."

The protagonist, however, receives the name "Robinson Crusoe"
from objects. He discovers it engraved on a shoulder strap by means
of which a sword is attached to his body. Only later does it become
clear that this is not really Robinson Crusoe, but a freed slave. Slowly,
he begins to inhabit the found name by relating to the objects of the
shipwreck. The ruins—mainly objects from Europe—become the first
fragments of his new identity.[2]

He then begins to appropriate the island. Words and characters
that arrived with the ship become instruments for the conquest of
"imperturbable being." They serve to order the chaos, to demarcate
a recognizable structure. Robinson Crusoe becomes master of his
world through the written characters. It is the European attitude of
conquest, appropriating the world though language and writing, that
breaks ground here: "I had retained the gift of speech; even the ability

---

1   Patrick Chamoiseau, *L'Empreinte à Crusoé*. Paris: Éditions Gallimard,
     2013, p. 292.
2   Ibid., p. 33.

to write; [...] after all these years I can say that I was happy, without vain hope, without shabby regrets, simply immaculate in my sovereign command over this small corner of the world; [...] I had become the founder of a civilization."[3]

Inaugurated by Western modernity, this vertical perspective—the rulers' view of things—has created an anthropocentric world. Now, at the beginning of the twenty-first century, this process—due to climate change, ocean acidification, and related developments—is destabilizing the planet and destroying large parts of the natural world, which is increasingly treated as a mere resource. Millions of people have been enslaved as cheap labor to harvest vegetable raw materials on the plantations. The expansion of Western rule over the planet has been a history of violence and oppression. Chamoiseau's Robinson Crusoe approaches the Caribbean island with the gaze and language of the European conqueror.

Yet, for the protagonist, the world changes fundamentally when he encounters "the trace of the other." This encounter "thrust me to the margin of this world like a discarded object; after having placed myself, at the end of these twenty years, at the center of everything."[4] He recognizes that the language, the signs he had used, belonged to an old, "rigid world." The order he had established through this traditional language had turned him into a fossil in a world which, although familiar and mastered, separated him from the riches surrounding him.

The moment he meets the other, the view shifts from the vertical to the horizontal. The ruler's linguistic order becomes visible as a prison: A new world view, that of Heraclitus, begins to assert itself. The rigid order dissolves; the world begins to move. The protagonist is no longer opposed to things, he becomes part of the world:

> "[I] now perceived [the island] as an effervescent disorder; the intruder was everywhere, invisible but highly intense; it was he who brought these landscapes, these butterflies, these scents, these enchanting lights into relief."[5]

3   Ibid., pp. 20–23.
4   Ibid., p. 73.
5   Ibid., p. 74.

He owes the expansion of his own world to the other's perspective. He learns to view the island as a "garden" and not as "property."[6] Thereby, he becomes part of this world to such an extent that the latter becomes animistically charged. In "exuberant" language, he combines plants, animals, and rocks: "[T]he trees suddenly came alive; they gathered together in secret assemblies";[7] "the noise of the birds emerged from indeterminacy, turning into chirping, whistling, piping, chattering and squawking."[8]

The discovery of the other on the island enables the protagonist to jettison the conqueror's world view and language—which had arrived by ship on the Caribbean island from Europe—and to develop his own language by engaging with the new world. The representation of a world from the vertical outside perspective is replaced by a language that arises from concrete, living interactions with the new world. It is a world of signs that develops wholly in the spirit of Caribbean philosopher Édouard Glissant, through a horizontal "relationality" with objects.[9]

Thus, Chamoiseau's protagonist moves between a linguistic order that turns out to be rigid and possessive on the one hand, and an irrepressible chaos in which life flourishes on the other. This movement also pervades the present first volume of our series *Das Neue Alphabet* (The New Alphabet).

The contribution "Perspective Cosmology and Digital Code" analyses the structure of the digital world: The binary code—the most abstract alphabet, based only on the distinction between two symbols—allows all other alphabets to be translated into the digital world. This is the basis of its efficacy, which, since the dawn of the twenty-first century, has generated a new form of capitalism, transforming all areas of life into commodities by converting them into digital code in order to monetize them. Thus, an unprecedented concentration of economic power and control was created. The binary code is historically rooted in the work of Gottfried Leibniz, who initially saw it as merely a means of dealing with the complexity of the

6   Ibid., p.130.
7   Ibid., p.113.
8   Ibid., p.111.
9   See also Édouard Glissant, *Caribbean Discourse: Selected Essays*, trans. Michael J. Dash. Charlottesville, VA and London: University of Virginia Press, 1989.

different world views with which the Baroque era was confronted. But while this resource triumphed in the twentieth century as a tool for world appropriation, the cosmology of perspectives, which enabled Leibniz to thematize the diversity of the world through manifold monadic modes of perception, was pushed into the background.

Following on from this contribution, Yuk Hui's "On the Cosmotechnical Nature of Writing" poses the fundamental question of whether we can reappropriate the New Alphabet—the digital code—and counter the global digital culture created by Silicon Valley with a greater diversity of different technologies. Opening a new space for thought to answer this question, he uses the example of Chinese script to show that technologies are not universal per se, but have to be understood from within their historical and cultural contexts. Leibniz himself, as Yuk Hui indicates, had already studied Chinese characters with great interest, not only because the hexagrams of the *I Ching* were similar to the binary code, but also because they could attain a high degree of expressiveness with only a limited number of visual symbols. Yuk Hui does not follow the common interpretation of Chinese characters as ideograms, instead regarding them as pictograms. This is because they do not refer to ideal forms, but to relations between things. Almost any sign can be broken down into parts that denote relationships between the things of the world and the cosmos. Historically, it was the art of the calligrapher to create these relations in search of the Dao. In this sense, writing is a cultural shaping of the world. This is the attitude that should be adopted when exploring the New Alphabet.

Ann Cotten weaves a thread between the different contributions of this volume. Her various text passages serve as "dewdrops," as she calls them in "表語文字—Gods, Logographs, and Dad Jokes." They reflect each other, as well as the other contributions, opening up closed meanings to new worlds: a representational strategy to break up monolithic meanings as they are evoked in the written language of the alphabet, in favor of a living, verbal culture. It is a method of undermining the determining role of the—mostly male—sender by embedding his statement in a stream of speech in which a multitude of voices is heard. In this respect, it is also a method to reclaim the linguistic multiplicity of meaning as a social practice: a multiplicity that has partly formed as a sediment in language itself, to be observed in homonyms. With words, once the wealth of signification—which unfolds in different contexts—has been recognized, they can no longer be understood as signs that unambiguously depict a world in the sense of representation. The task is rather to work with words in a complex world. Similar to Yuk Hui, Ann Cotten thus develops a counter-image to the one-dimensional understanding of language, which, as in the case for digital-platform capitalism, generates forms of structural violence.

If Ann Cotten's textual pieces transform the signs of this volume into a stream of reflecting units, Ben Lerner's two contributions can be read as overarching frames for the texts assembled here. In the first, he recounts how, as a child, he learned the letters of the alphabet through the "Alphabet Song." The song appears as a sensual technology facilitating the internalization of the characters. The alphabet provides the poet with a powerful system for ordering the world: "the order of orders." If an ordering system such as the alphabet is needed to be able to articulate anything at all, the knowledge of the meaning of a word congeals language. The moment the meaning of a word is fixed, it can still function, but it loses its vitality. It is the task of poetry—as Ben Lerner states in his second contribution—to use words in such a way that their meanings remain in limbo, always unfolding anew in the interaction between participants.

Wolfgang Tillmans' digital-image world unfolds alongside the texts of the language world. The project *Neue Welt* presented here was created following a twenty-year period, during which he took photos with a thirty-five-millimeter analogue camera, a Contax SLR with a fifty-millimeter lens. The brand was discontinued in 2004, and in 2009 Tillmans started working with a digital camera. While the analogue years had been characterized by the examination of the medium of film—the aesthetic exploration of the reaction of photographic paper to light, the effects of mechanical and chemical processes—Tillmans now used digital technology to visually explore the outside world all over again. But the medium had fundamentally changed. Digital technology led to an image sharpness and density of information that far exceeded analogue photography. This resulted in an excess of information, which constantly challenged, even overwhelmed, viewers. The medium thus creates a perception that corresponds to this permanent information overload, through what Tillmans calls the "HD world," with the implication that the "HD world" is in fact our world. Yet it is not only his use of the digital medium that corresponds to our condensed and accelerated present, but also his travels all over the world. It is a journey across continents to well-known, as well as more remote, places. In the context of his project *Neue Welt*, Tillmans stayed only briefly at the places he was visiting, pursuing his interest in exploring surfaces, because, as he says, one can read the "truth of things" from them.

Due to the transformation of the Earth system, the growing mobility and interconnectedness of societies, the forced migration of entire population groups, and—as has recently become apparent— the outbreak of pandemics (whose unforeseeable psychosocial effects trigger a stage of unprecedented uncertainty), our living environments are becoming increasingly complex. By contrast, new technologies are enforcing an international standardization in the form of a homogenization driven by scaling, and we are witnessing the attempt of new nationalisms to mobilize complex social developments through policies driven by stereotypes and linguistic reductionisms.

Against this background, Das Neue Alphabet sees itself as a project in which medial techniques of representation are thematized and developed in order to do justice to the complexity of our situation. This will involve navigating between a multitude of not-completely-understood phenomena, resistant observations and experiences, and the ever-new attempt to create networks of relationships and patterns. It is a movement between cosmos and chaos, in which the potential for violence emanating from planetary developments is revealed, and the potential possibilities manifested in chaos are articulated in terms of the social production of meaning.

Bernd Scherer,
Director of the Haus der Kulturen der Welt

Translated from the German by Kevin Kennedy

ABCs:
A Holiday Card for
Alexander Kluge

'I cannot sing,' he answered, 'and that is why I came hither
from the feast.' But he who spake unto him said, 'Sing the
beginning of created things.' Thereupon Caedmon began to
sing verses that he had never heard before, of this import:
'Now should we praise the power and wisdom of the Creator,
the works of the Father.' This is the sense but not the form
of the hymn that he sang while sleeping.
—William J. Long, *English Literature* (1909)

The first song I remember learning is the *Alphabet Song*, also known as
the *ABCs*. It is set to a melody that originates in an anonymous French
pastoral song from 1740. It became the melody of the French song *Ah!
vous dirai-je, maman*, which was then popularized through Mozart's
12 Variations. The song *Twinkle, Twinkle, Little Star*—also one of the
first songs an English-speaking child learns—is set to the same music.
I only realized this two months ago, when it was pointed out to me by
my daughter's kindergarten teacher. Even though I can understand
in the abstract that these are the same melodies, I cannot experience
them as identical. It's as though the *Alphabet Song* is so fundamental
that I'm unable to scrape the lyrics off the music in order to see that
it's also the structure that underpins *Twinkle, Twinkle, Little Star*. Trying to think the music independent of the alphabet lyrics is like trying
to imagine prelinguistic consciousness; my mind goes blank, goes
quiet. The music is supposedly an aid to memory, but the mnemonic
has fused with its object so thoroughly it induces a kind of forgetting
of the melody as such. I probably knew other songs well before the
Alphabet Song, but in my recollection it is primary. Singing it with my
mother under the green glow-in-the-dark plastic stars I'd stuck to my
bedroom ceiling.

The song is simple and profound: First you name the letters, and
the names of the letters in English are the letters. After "and z," after
all the letters have been activated, the singer is capable of arranging
them into speech: "Now I know my ABCs." Now that I have named the
building blocks of expression I am I: the first person, the nominative

singular pronoun. I wasn't I until *now*, I am emerging from language. "Next time won't you sing with me"—now that I am I, I can open out to the social, imagine you, whoever you are, and the possibility that song might be shareable, communal; I can join the feast. (This is what innumerable poems, maybe all poems, say: a language, a social world precedes me, forms me, and now I call out in it; who can hear me, sing with me—perhaps transform it?) In this sense the *Alphabet Song* is the song of songs.

The ritual song naturalizes the alphabet. It ensures that when I actually learn to write, to represent letters graphically, I will experience it as anamnesis—alphabetization will feel like remembering, because this technology of writing was preprogrammed by song. I will less acquire than recall the aid to memory writing is. The song will also make the order of the alphabet itself appear natural, immutable as the heavens. The song will emphasize the rhymes of the long "e" sounds—C/D, G, P, V, Z—both so I can memorize the letters and so their order will feel inevitable. But why is the English alphabet ordered as it is? Mere historical precedent. Unlike with numbers, there is no logical or essential sequence to the letters, and knowing alphabetical order does not help one read or write. The alphabet is the order of orders, pure convention that song transforms into social necessity. You cannot be a social singer until you recite the letters in the order your culture has ordained. And other orders are enforced by this one. "A is for Apple," we are taught, the fruit of knowledge, the fall into time, into difference, into arbitrary signs.

When I was a child at a small synagogue in Topeka, Kansas, they told us a story of a Rabbi who comes upon a boy who is supposed to be praying. But instead of praying, the Rabbi discovers, the boy is reciting the Hebrew alphabet. The Rabbi asks the child to account for himself and he explains that since only God is capable of composing a prayer worthy of God, he's offering up the alphabet with the idea that God can use it to make the prayer that will suffice—that will transcend the limitations of the created and be worthy of the creator who preceded it. (Only in a dream can Caedmon find the worthy form.)

The first letter of Hebrew—a new old language, like a temple that has been rebuilt, or a city reconstructed after an aerial bombing—is *aleph*, and makes no sound. Spinoza said *aleph* is the sign of "the beginning of sound in the throat that is heard by its opening." According to Daniel Heller-Roazen, Spinoza is still assigning it too much sound: "Aleph guards the place of oblivion at the inception of every alphabet." It is a letter that stands for a sound everyone has always forgotten, must forget in order to speak, a sound only a God could make. A sound survived by its letter like a star survived by its light.

Stars don't actually twinkle. What we experience as variations in their brightness is just perturbation in the medium. Twinkle, twinkle, little star / How I wonder what you are. Now I know my ABCs, and can sing beneath them of created things. What precedes the alphabet no I can say.

14   Kanako Tada: *Valleygirl* 只只只 (see p. 54)

只
只只
只只

しかく 四角 只 照 く
詩客 資格 只
鹿 食う まる れ 参る 冈。ぱ
です。三角 絡 椿 鹿岳 酸 シ さんずい
再 入 苻 最終 参加 者 食う
採 集 鹿 集
住つ 松 末
疲 土 せ 又 労 唐 怒 度 !! 足
do（ 仍 月 土 日 曜 何 処 土 語
誰 ？

イロハ

The *Alphabet Song* brings to mind the *Iroha*, which one could, were one so inclined, call the Japanese *Alphabet Song*. It is a song that features each of the syllables of the language once, and which was used as an (arbitrary) sequence for counting, calculation, dictionaries, and so on, just like the alphabet.

以呂波耳本部止
千利奴流乎和加
餘多連曽津祢那
良牟有為能於久
耶万計不己衣天
阿佐伎喩女美之
恵比毛勢須

The *Iroha* first featured in the 金光明最勝王経音義 (*konkômyô-saishôôkyôongi* / Readings of Golden Light Sutra) of 1079. It was written in 万葉仮名 (man'yôgana), an ancient writing system first documented in the 万葉集 (*Man'yôshū*), a Japanese poetry anthology from the Nara period. Chinese characters are used as a writing system for the Japanese language—this was the first known syllabic kana system of the Japanese language, in use since at least the midseventh century.

Texts in this system also use Chinese characters for their meaning, but 万葉仮名 refers only to characters in phonetic use. The phonetic values were derived from the contemporary Chinese pronunciation, though, at the same time, native Japanese readings of the character were also in use. For example, 木 (tree) is read as "moku" or "ki"/"ko". Thus the double reading of the 万葉集 has been conserved to this day, as most contemporary Kanji have a "Chinese" and a "Japanese" reading. Simplified versions of 万葉仮名 eventually gave rise to both the ひらがな (hiragana) and カタカナ (katakana) scripts used in Modern Japanese. In a way, learning about 万葉仮名 feels like going back to before a fork in the road.

Structurally the poem follows the standard 7-5 pattern of Japanese poetry, and is usually is written out that way in these paper-affluent times. The text of the poem in modern hiragana (with archaic ゐ *wi* and ゑ *we*, which are now only used in proper names and certain Okinawan orthographies, but without voiced consonant marks) is:

Classical Japanese		Modern Japanese		Translation
いろはにほへと	Iro ha nihoheto	色は匂えて	Iro wa nioedo	These coloured flowers*
ちりぬるを	Chirinuru wo	散りぬるを	Chirinuru o	will soon be scattered.
わかよたれぞ	Wa ka yo tare so	我が世誰ぞ	Wa ga yo dare zo	In our world, who
つねならむ	Tsune naramu	常ならん	Tsune naran	can fail to change?
うゐのおくやま	Uwi no okuyama	有為の奥山	Ui no okuyama	This mountain of real affairs,
けふこえて	Kefu koete	今日越えて	Kyô koete	pass through it today,
あさきゆめみし	Asaki yume mishi	浅き夢見じ	Asaki yume miji	without shallow dreams
ゑひもせす	Wehi mo sesu	酔いもせず	ei mo sezu	nor drunk on ideas.

*   In an example of collective synesthesia, the meaning of the word niou
         has shifted over the centuries from the old Japanese meaning of visual shin-
         ing to the modern meaning of having an (often unpleasant) odor.
         The many poems about flowers may have played a role in this movement.

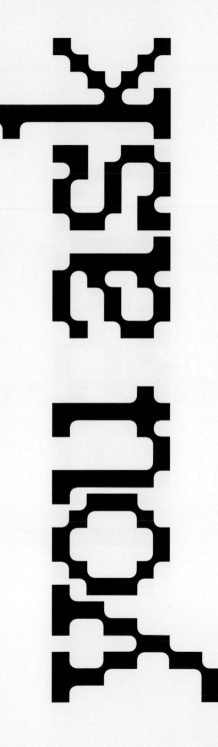

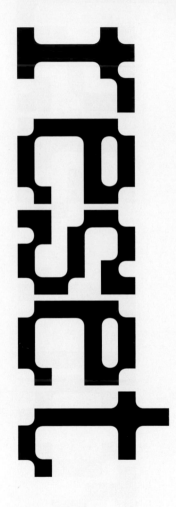

An English translation by Professor Ryuichi Abe reads:

> Although its scent still lingers on
> the form of a flower has scattered away
> For whom will the glory of this world remain unchanged?
> Arriving today at the yonder side
> of the deep mountains of evanescent existence
> We shall never allow ourselves to drift away
> intoxicated, in the world of shallow dreams.

Afternote: What a strange, melancholy thrill comes with reading a text—or, for that matter, a building, a path, a skill—from long in the past. How wildly sexy and anarchic such age also is! German magic fragments that stuck in my mind, warped and falsified, like "firiwizza master," in English "spring is icumen in." The German text I was taught about in high school, but the first Old English texts I discovered in anthologies of English verse, with no didactics hovering around to tell me where to put them. The text seemed to buckle alive from the page as I smelled the morphological development of my language, and it spoke to my pheromones, and I suppose I thought I could also change its curve.

The author thanks Prof. Urs Matthias Zachmann for advice and teaching.

表語文字―
Gods, Logographs,
and Dad-Jokes

The foreign learner sees homonyms. She looks in the Japanese-English dictionary and sees, for example:

歴史	rekishi	history
轢死	rekishi	being run over

And she thinks—wooo! ... and she thinks—what does she *want* to think? Something funny, maybe? She is just some Joseph looking for a manger and would like to find the joke of all jokes. She likes the idea that deep in the generative transformation grammar of humanity lies a huge, productive pun that originally brought forth us all? (What a *feminine* thought, isn't it. You get born as a girl and keep thinking: No, this has to be a joke. They can't be serious.)

What is she looking for? That is probably what she will find. Just like Darwin, looking at animals he did not know well on faraway islands, saw the structures and not the animals, the network of overlap and wordplay that makes those familiar with the language sigh or wince shows to the foreigner some shadow of a skeleton structure that is less apparent to her in her own language. She has come in from somewhere else with all senses a-tremble and a structuralist *idée fixe*.

And the pun-loather—whose discrimination I aspire to—is like: "Duh, what is so *interesting* about homonymy?" And something about this lying prostrate with this sensitivity and *idée fixe* under the stern brow of the pun despiser excites me. I have *futile knowledge*. Maybe, also, I am encouraged by the analogy to the world we live in, which has been carefully designed in the past years to ensure consumers can pass by the production sites and producers of their end products without putting two and two together.

What is so interesting about homonymy? I can't quite explain if you don't feel the same boundless delight about the fact that the same sound means something *completely different* in a different context! Something with *no connection!* I think that is just so beautiful! The two words sounding alike is not the symptom of a connection, quite on the contrary, it shows how unconnected the spheres are in which they were formed. If there had ever been any likelihood of them being confused, they would have needed a disambiguation sign.

Either that, or else speaking has to occur between people with the possibility of a short dialogue to clarify such little confusions—a dialogue that can create a moment of diplomatic warmth and cooperativity, like a chat about the weather, with which language has in common that all users suffer it together. It also reminds me of the ubiquity of people named Mohammed in some countries (in others people named Lena...). These somewhat helpless repetitions of formal identity seem to say: Names may not be as important as they seem.

English too has more synonyms and homonyms than German, and correspondingly, punning in English has the reputation of producing groans (while in German, *Wortspiel* is a fairly neutral word). In Japan more even than in English, the Old Man's Wordplay or dad joke, the *ohyaji-gyaggu*, based on one of the millions of puns waiting in the dictionaries for the gullible wit, is feared and dreaded like a fart. Conversely, in daily life there is a constant, rather pleasant atmosphere of cooperation in disambiguation and differentiation, even on TV. It is all in the spirit of the serious, not the Anglo and German "Not-true-Jokes," the pleasant humour comes from a slight amusement about the way the world is so confoundable—amusement like a springy bed without someone coming and jumping on it, pleasure like looking at a beautiful picture without someone coming and explaining it... you get the idea.

If you have read Kobo Abe's *The Woman in the Dunes*, you will remember how the village works together to keep up the daily work of shoveling clear the sand holes in which the houses have been enveloped, and there is no escaping, since it would be very ugly behaviour to leave the others. Similarly endless collective maintenance work seems to be done on the language, the fine differentiations of the words eroding constantly into an ignorance that will become dangerous when it is too late. Like the dune, language is of immense scale and superhuman beauty.

We live in a complex world where things can easily be confused; we must work together to make it a coherent place to live. What a different conception of language, compared to to the anagrammatic square-dancing virtuosity cultivated in a poetic sphere where the unusual—*das Neue*—gains points simply for being new and this single leftover criterion has become inflationary; where for some reason people seem to be bored with subtle and acute use of truth and sense because their world has become so reduced, so that the goal has become to confuse any reader, or to impress xem, taking the brain on wild rides between sound, meaning, and space. Which is trippy, but may also leave you alone shivering, a useless person on a trampled garden, once the electricity for the music of the *special* is gone.

Something interesting happens for literature when language is already so rich. It happens a bit in English (having many times as much vocabulary as, say, German), but is massive in Chinese or Japanese: When word play, that bizarrely networked, crass poetry, is done automatically by the language already, the point of good literature becomes a matter of taste in choosing *which* sonic, poetic connections to amplify with each other, to what point. If, then, to Japanese or Chinese poets,the emphasis on freedom in poorer languages' poetics can be enticing for a sweet moment of *freedom from* the weight of their brocade language, I also feel with them a certain distress about how to bury their fine sense of taste, which depends on the situation. Set beside Chinese and Japanese literature, Europe's celebration of liberation—from quite unnecessary, stupid constraints—seems clunky and medieval. There have also always been quiet, rich local cultures here too, mossy growths of habits, mythologies, jokes, styles, but these rural, regional, and dialectal phenomena have been traditionally excluded from the world of the written word, much to its impoverishment. First, the Catholic Church killed the local spirits with the cross, then Protestantism killed off the ones that were still hiding in the guise of Saints. We have been educated in a cultural desert.

The European notion of individuality also suffers from colonial history, which is characterised by the habit of universalising the speaker's own smallness. We measure the universe by multiplying our small scope—Europe being, for example, at least ten times smaller on the map than in our heads—and always imagine the universe much too small also. Only in such a shrunken universe could one hang one's ambition on being unique. Cultures with better mathematical imagery also have better music that helps school the mind as well—we have nothing better than Mozart; beloved as he is, he and Bach are not exactly Gamelan polyphony. Many cultures on this Earth, and often the smaller ones, know without having to think twice that the universe is not just infinite, but infinite times infinite—the difference lying in the knowledge that there are endless versions of myself out there, and that therefore I am banal. And being friendly with this existential feeling. It is not tragic, it is more like a saving grace: It means simply to participate in an endless melody, as long and wide as nature. And this is definitely not ONE "god" with any kind of facial hair, but, dearies, it is also not an abstract idea of unity. In my experience, it is more like there are concentrations of specificity in particular nooks all over the place, local spirits, ghosts, and the like, all explainable with quantum theory if one could only follow it, but which may have a perfectly mathematical Quark-like tendency to elude explanation. Explanation as we have learned to enjoy it being tailored to the kind of control and representation that has been most successful in the industrial era, but which we are outgrowing—precisely in the measure that the explanations necessary to explain, for example, human behavior exceed in length the lifespan of any one human being—throwing us straight back to place-holders like the mystifying terms we used in olden days. The purely quantitative problem of translating everything into steam punk causal models is where my "pick your mystic model" attitude hails from.

There is no canon, no one holy WORD, except maybe the hydrogen molecule. Even the hydrogen molecule is only the illusion of a dragon carried by atoms in black stage suits. Water only begins to be watery when there is a huge multiplication of molecules. So my intuition doubts the perspicuity of projecting a narration of growth in analogy to animals' cell division onto the whole universe, and I prefer to concentrate on a differentiation occurring on a blow-up in which expansion means dilution, and dilution means more space for the specificities to unfold. (Obviously, both being just guides for imagination of unimaginable processes.) To gain understanding of a reality in which one is unimportant is to lose one's grip in things one believed to own and control—(as the analytic philosophers do say: to hold a belief).

The fact of infinite infinities also changes the conception of individuality. I can yearn to be an exception, or else I can feel how interesting, how readable one is as a recombination of elements. Others are fascinating, and I can relate to them because they are recombinations of the same elements and patterns I also am a version of. This linguistic cosmology shifts the focus from being ununderstood to being understandable—an essential point for a poet.

There is, for example, in Buddhist mythology, the image of Indra's net, where dewdrops hang at the intersections of an endless web, each drop reflecting all other drops. The drops that mirror each other are, at the same time, the same and different already by being identical, but in a position shifted by one. It means the whole universe applies to each of us and thus unites us, cradles us in its infinite variety that is not stuck to any individual being. We, these beings, can slip around in this network, insofar as we are reading heads, or little ribosomes of making sense, hiccupping, usually harmless sources of reproduction and error.

This soothing image liberates me from the stress of deciding with my own limited knowledge on respect or disrespect for all those *other* things out there, like some kind of judge. I no longer have to, with my own mental muscle, heave and import each new bit of information into my bag of world knowledge, and set it down in the card registry system with the right connections. The world is out there, and anything new I encounter is sure to echo in some way, connect with what I know, without me having to compare, ascribe, evaluate, or appropriate its existence. I can also keep my thoughts to myself, as they are just incomplete echoes of the universe, not unique little embryos that will wither and die if not carried into the world and coded onto paper. I do not have to *acquire* (and then stake a claim to and slap copyright on) all things that exist on Earth in order to have a place. I am connected from birth and need only discover. And the discovery also does not "fill up" my consciousness like my useless vocabulary notebooks; instead my perception of the universe grows more and more differentiated as I learn from the endlessly varied, but also endlessly repetitive society that flows through my movements. I am the Mohammed of this house, the young Mohammed, the old Mohammed, Mohammed the mother, the sister, the brother, the father, the mother's brother, et cetera. Just like "I" will mean so many things in the course of a life. Changing, I recognise myself as the node of everything and everyone I know, and I know myself in the mirrors of their recognition. Taken from this context, I am undefined and have no meaning as I walk down the street. Which can be as nice as sleep, but also as sad as dying.

Back to language. Not only must Kanji be learnt in context, if one does not intend to sink into a quicksand of Onyomi and Kunyomi, like a sabertoothed tiger in a tar swamp. Japanese is, like English, a language in which, instead of making the words carry around little signs to mark their gender, case, and number, these things are left to context and word order. Making for a smooth flow and less acrobatic self-defining among the words. The sense of a word is not a Frankenstein's Monster of fragments of meaning collected over time by a speaker in little word-boxes, as sketched in valence theories, but more like the movement in use that may surround a tool. Or like the "meaning" of musical chords, seasons, paths: conjured up more by dynamic context, the postures and movements of the words toward each other, among one another. Meaning occurs when several words come together, like a chatty atmosphere or an electrical current, and disappears again when the words are isolated. And thus it does not happen quite as easily that someone forces words on others or forces words to do something paradox.

On the other hand, people may be forced to fake one half of the conventional cooperative conversation in such situations, which can be more painful than waiting for a mansplainer to finish while one checks one's emails on one's phone. In the USA, I was warned not to force people in dependent situations, like students or service personnel, to laugh at my jokes—ooh, I feel the pain in this very moment, I feel like a sadistic, sad stand-up comedian at an open mic, taking five minutes revenge on xeir audience. In Japan, a certain pathos surrounds the traditional practice of two or more people alternating blows with a pestle or hammer, rhythmicising and collectivising tedious work. If one of them goes independent, serious injuries may ensue. But the same rhythms can be found in comedy. (While, like here, the bourgeois politely and formally wait for each individual person to finish whatever bullshit they feel they need to say.) Similar fast, codependent techniques can be found in the polyrhythms of West Africa or Indonesia's Gamelan music. I mean to say, that is also language's way, unlike systems like biblical rhetoric or French post-structuralist theory, which in their linear hypnoses seem to derive from competitive ball games with the goal of *preventing* the *opponent* from getting the ball. It seems tastelessly reckless, recklessly blind to behave that way in many cultures and subcultures of this world. If you look, for example, at chat etiquette—well, I suppose that depends. In some places it seems to be the fashion to send off tiny bites of chat over a while, so the phone of the receiver keeps binging merrily; other people prefer that one formulate what one has to say and say it all in one go—forfeiting, of course, the possibility of a slow and gentle fade in of an idea with feedback from the other. This need for constant feedback has been marked as a behavior trait of young females in the wake of "Valley girl talk" or "high rising terminals" but it is also a rhythmic feature of hip-hop intros, cowboy grunts, and other situations where it seems appropriate to get in the groove before one unpacks one's preconceived thoughts. And it is an art.

So the good habits of some oral cultures have been terrorised and endangered by the written culture that has been so automatically seen as more "highly" developed. But my rant in *this* place can serve only to offer the alphabeticised tribes some helpful advice for survival.

The two models remain significant for the tragedy of class history: There are those who instinctively feel the need to create some kind of harmony or harmony in fight culture or whatever, in any room, some kind of micro-justice in the atmosphere. Shall we call them the Mothers? Or the Long-term Non-annoying Coworkers? And there are others who come into a space and are led by their instincts to try to dominate it, by subterfuge or by brute force of voice space, and who often don't even notice how silly they are because the work-force is so polite.

My academic point is that the model of communication (sender) (receiver) (topic) or (denoted/denoting) the way we learned it at university is NOT universal. One-way communication is not equally prevalent in all cultures and regions. And that is one of the reasons why some regions came to be colonised—they were being too polite, too cooperative in their conversational style. The one-sided communication form of written culture has taken over the world and secured it for industrial-scale harassment and destruction.

FUCK the alphabet.

Talk given at Alexander Kluge's exhibit, 2019/1/10, Haus der Kulturen der Welt, Berlin

Cosmology of
Perspectives and Digital Code

Having evolved over generations, our notions of reality are now being turned upside down. The world we live in is undergoing a fundamental transformation. We encounter taxi firms without a fleet of vehicles and companies that don't possess rooms but offer accommodation. We purchase goods from retail chains that are already aware of what we wish to buy. We are bemused by cars without steering wheels, motoring driverless on the roads. New business models are emerging, and existing power structures are shifting.[1]

Via the new media, we are witnessing an excessive growth in the body of knowledge to which we are afforded access. At the same time, our traditional categories and concepts no longer serve to help us understand this transformation and thus to participate in the social discourse.

These trends are driven by a capitalism that avails itself of the predictability provided by the digital technologies, which are leveraging a specific development in the concept of alphabets. Alphabets are characterized by their finite number of discrete and therefore distinct characters. The highest level of abstraction found in alphabets is represented by the binary code. It comprises just two distinguishing symbols, 1 and 0, which have no intrinsic significance. The binary code facilitates the segmentation of the analogue continuum into discrete and therefore computational units. As a formal language, it can be operated by machines.

The machines of the digital world operate on the basis of algorithms. Algorithms break down operations into single steps and stipulate the routines that operate with these elements, based on a specific, predetermined schema. This explains why it is not necessary for the person or machine using the schema to understand what they are doing. The operation is purely physical in nature. The binary code provides the symbols the machine must read in order to implement the algorithms. All decisions are taken at the coding level—within the operational processes, everything is predetermined; there are no decisions to be made.

---

1 The corona crisis has demonstrated just how fragile those notions of reality are—in terms of both health and economic activity. What the medium- and long-term effects are, remains to be seen.

The binary code was developed during the Baroque period by Gottfried Wilhelm Leibniz (1646–1716) in order to facilitate a machine-based approach to solving mathematical problems. Perhaps it is no coincidence that close scrutiny of our own age reveals many similarities to the Baroque era. During the Baroque, the global process of exchange became established for the first time in history. Under the then politically and economically asymmetrical power structures, silver from Latin America was exchanged for enslaved people from Africa and silk from China. European ships brought commodities from across the globe to Europe.

Along with the exponential growth in the flow of goods, there was a veritable explosion in our body of knowledge. The cabinets of curiosity were constantly being filled with new objects—as yet uncategorized and unnamed. It was a time characterized by excessive accumulation of both material and knowledge, which often lay outside the existing modes of thought and systems of classification. In addition to the curiosity cabinets, academic institutes such as the Royal Society in London or the Académie française in Paris were established in 1660 and 1635 respectively. Their founding mission was to debate, classify, and evaluate knowledge. As associations of experts, the academies were expected to furnish society with access to, and an orientation in, these new worlds.

The philosopher who elaborated both a praxis and a theoretical model for navigating this world was the very same Leibniz who invented the binary code. In his *Monadology*, he developed a theoretical system based on a cosmology of perspectives. This cosmology is made up of bodies: monads that form one unit. It is a world in which all bodies are interrelated and react to each other. The monads are the perceptions through which the external world is represented internally. Due to the potential bond uniting one unit in the world with the others, each single monad reflects the entire world, and consequently each monad has a universal perspective. Universalism, therefore, is not located on the level of objects, but on the level of perception. It invariably offers a view onto the entire world, but also from a particular perspective, a particular universalism. Within Leibniz's cosmology of perspectives, there is never one entire ontological overview of the world, but always and only partial insights.

And this is where the praxis of Leibniz begins. It is a praxis intended to facilitate the inter-exchange of perspectives. For example, he cultivated an exchange of letters and manuscripts with over a hundred correspondents across the world. Under his theoretical model of monadology, each correspondent constitutes a monad in possession of its own worldview or perspective. To Leibniz, the academies being founded during this time were simply monads of a higher level, on which they were unifying to formulate a common worldview. As worldviews are invariably particular, they are also negotiable; no one can claim to have an invariant, universal knowledge—not even the academies.

Of greater import is that monadology does not require the dualistic categorization of the nascent modernity. Not only people are perceived as monads, but also animals and machines—for they too possess perceptions. In their interaction with human beings, they assume an active role, even if their perspectives are, according to Leibniz, not located on the same level as those of humans. He thus posited a cosmology that assigned to non-human creatures an active role in the process of world-creation. And he went a step further: Even the parts of the human body—hands, feet, and so on—are in themselves monads. This allows him to attribute to these parts their own perceptual processes. Consequently, according to Leibniz, our hands and feet possess their own perceptions and, by extension, ways of accessing the world—an insight that plays a fundamental role in today's sensor technology.

In his monadology, Leibniz developed a cosmology that facilitated a modeling of the manifold knowledge-production processes of his age. At the same time, however, he fashioned an instrument and a praxis that enabled the representation of knowledge. Through correspondence with the Jesuits in China—where his principal interest lay in the pictographic script used by the Chinese—he developed this instrument to serve the praxis of monadology. Yet, beyond a classification system, as was also developed by Raimundus Lullus for example, his other chief objective was to establish a formalism in the representation of all available knowledge. His basic idea was an "alphabet of human thought" in which all existing ideas are derived from just a handful of fundamental concepts, which are assigned simple character elements. The formation of complex concepts, and thus the generation of an entire body of knowledge, is performed subsequently as a character operation predicated on the rules of a calculus.

Here, Leibniz was able to take recourse to a crucial discovery of his own. As mentioned above, he had already invented the binary code, which subsequently was to become the foundation for digitization. His characters serve as the basic symbols for representing the entire arithmetic in one calculus. A calculus comprises one basic figure and a set of basic rules, which allow for the production of more complex characters. And using this fundamental constellation, all operations can be performed by a machine. Leibniz applied this procedure to the entire body of knowledge. Since in his universal language program (the *characteristica universalis*) the basic signs were connected to his fundamental basic concepts, all the concepts of our knowledge could be generated from these basic concepts by calculation—thus creating an alphabet of thought. Leibniz then went a step further by applying this procedure to sentences in order to generate all possible true sentences through calculus.

Understanding the link between monadology and the *characteristica universalis* was decisive for the further development of knowledge. By means of these characters, the universal language generated in the calculus refers to concepts, and thus to already objectified knowledge. It expresses the knowledge of a specific time and has the capacity to reveal certain relationships that are not immediately apparent. This attained crucial significance during the Baroque era, as our body of knowledge literally exploded. Here, the "knowledge alphabet" provides an instrument to aid navigation through the constantly expanding worlds of knowledge. In contrast, the monadology is a model for examining how knowledge is generated in the first place. The answer: through the perspectives, the forms of perception of the monads, whereby the perspectives of the monads are reflections of all aspects of one monad in interaction with all the others.

Viewed against the backdrop of the Leibniz program, the current situation of digital capitalism can be described as one in which the model of monadological knowledge production is being increasingly displaced by the instrument of the alphabetization of knowledge, which is predicated on the objectification of knowledge. Supplanting the knowledge society is the "extractive society."

Fundamentally, this process consists of dividing up the world into the smallest possible discrete units, to be fed into the machines of the digital world as data. These units are generated as data in the digitization process, under which the continuous physical world is segmented into discrete units as in the binary code. For instance, an analogue photograph is digitized when it is transformed into a file, which is made up of grid-like points or pixels, to which a color value is then assigned.

This example shows how, by means of digitization, a world of data is created and facilitates the expression of our world of experience with the aid of a formal syntax. At the same time, a diverse array of media, images, tones, type sets, and so on, can be represented across the same level. All information is separated into the smallest basic units, which can then be combined freely. These units are not monads in the Leibniz sense of the word, but separate, discrete segmented objects, devoid of any system of reference.

Monadological knowledge-production processes only feature in the determination of the discrete units—as is the case in the process of programming, which is performed by experts. The units of data are now already objectified knowledge, and the routines performed by the machines are of a purely physical nature. Consequently, it is crucial to understand how these basic units are generated and the role played by programming.

In discussions on understanding what life is, the determination of these fundamental units assumes a highly controversial role. Concurrent with the secularization of key areas of society, many scientists began to harbor the dream of humankind creating life itself. Their project underwent its first florescence in the kitchens of the Renaissance and Baroque alchemists. Via the Faustian myth of the eighteenth century and the figure of Frankenstein in the early nineteenth century, these notions entered into the cultural memory. And today, they are experiencing a renewed revival in the digitized technological landscape of California, where dreams range from the creation of particularly intelligent life forms—or prolonging life or even achieving eternal life—to the so-called technological singularity: an omniscient technological entity that outperforms human intelligence and therefore has no need for it anymore.

This revival is attributable essentially to the close links between biology on the one hand, and information science and digital technology on the other, which appear to hold the genuine prospect of intervening fundamentally in life itself. This relationship, however, has itself only been made possible by a specific definition of the basic unit of life and, by extension, of what life actually is.

The determination of the basic unit of life traces back to the early twentieth century, when Darwin's evolutionary theory was combined with Gregor Mendel's theory of genetics. This led to genetic differentiation being identified as an explanation of Darwin's concept of natural selection. Genetic information is carried by the chromosomes, which are an essential part of the cell structure. In sexual reproduction, the germ cells protect the chromosomes, thus enabling—according to theory—the self-reproduction of the organism. In essence, life appears to be defined by the basic genetic structure. This concept gained greater credence in the 1950s with the discovery of the stability and self-producing properties of DNA.

Initially, however, it was not clear that DNA was a genetic code. This theory only emerged from the contemporaneous research into cybernetics, information theory, and computer science, which started to confirm the interpretation of DNA as a self-regulating communications system that transmitted information via the proteins. The answer to the question "What is life?" was thus unequivocal: "Life is information." The objective of the research was to decipher the alphabet of life in the form of DNA (the acronym of Das Neue Alphabet alludes to DNA). This ultimately paved the way for the Human Genome Project—one of the flagship Big Science projects.

Underpinning this entire development was initially the ability to identify DNA as the foundation of life, and subsequently to read this as a code and exploit the discreteness of the alphabet, which allowed basic units to be machine-processed as data. It was the prodigious processing power of modern computers that then enabled the code to be cracked. This breakthrough was accompanied by the belief that the foundations were now in place to be able in future to not only "read" life but also to technologically manipulate it, for example by isolating genes deemed responsible for specific diseases. By virtue of the computer, life had become operationalized.

The Human Genome Project highlighted just how many basic assumptions flow into the construction of the smallest units, which, now as data and thus objectified objects, serve as the foundation for computational operations in the world of machines, which started to fundamentally reshape our understanding of the world.

In recent years, however, these basic assumptions have been cast into doubt, as it has become increasingly obvious that the genome is not a separable basic unit from which life can be generated in complete isolation. On the contrary, it is embedded within a network of interactive relationships, integrated into both natural and historical processes. Not only is the cell the historical product of free-living bacteria, but DNA is also partly of viral origin. Consequently, human evolution is inconceivable without this encounter with these viruses and the interaction with bacteria. Therefore, the focus now should be directed at the ecological relationship between diverse actors, rather than on one individual object. The genome is not a fundamental unit in the Leibniz sense, but rather a monad or a partial human monad embedded within a variety of interactive relations. To understand life, therefore, it is necessary to focus on the dynamics of these interaction processes. This would signify, however, that life is no longer directly manipulable through technological operations—the premise upon which the Genome Project is predicated.

The history of science through to the Genome Project shows how infinitely diverse extracts of the world and of life can be separated into discrete units on the basis of scientific theory. According to Leibniz, the world is reproduced from specific perspectives by interrupting a potentially infinite process of division at a certain juncture in order to generate discreteness. These perspectives are no longer present in the final outcome of this process, in our case the genome; they are declared as an invariant, that is, indistinguishable and thus objectified.

This example also shows that the most diverse assumptions flow into such a process, among them the notion that the world is constructed from the smallest units, from which everything can then be generated. But if, in order to understand life, we must consider entire ecologies involving many actors, when does it make sense, at least in the realm of life, to operate with such units?

Attention has until now only been directed at the knowledge aspect of this process, in which these fundamental units are objectified. However, this process also contains an economic dimension. For, under digital capitalism, the objectification of life, its reduction to discrete and thus manipulable data, also facilitates commodification.

In this way, digital technology is impinging on analogue reality, in the process forging complex psycho- and socio-technological living environments. But the system of reference framed by Big Data between the individual data sets is, by the same token, not monadic. For this fundamental process entails simply breaking down existing reality into the smallest possible units, out of which entire new worlds can then be constructed. Which particular worlds are to be built is contingent upon how the machines are programmed. Knowledge processes are being fed into the system, akin to Leibniz's monadic perceptions. As such, they invariably reflect only particular extracts of the world, which under the monadology theory would then be societally negotiated. De facto, however, they are already excluded from the social discourse by virtue of their division into discrete objects and are increasingly dictated by market or state interests.

Yet, they not only reflect these interests but also other societal power structures, such as prejudicially racist or gender-specific structures that are inscribed into the categorization of the programs. The crucial factor here is that these categorizations—which, by virtue of their objectification, are disbarred from the social discourse—create worlds by writing themselves into the societal processes. In place of the knowledge society—in which, according to the monadology theory, everyone is participating in the production of knowledge, each from their own particular perspective—the so-called "extractive society" has established itself through the instrument of digitization and the attendant implicit objectification and commodification processes.

Digital infrastructures also essentially control the infrastructures with which we are rebuilding the planet—from the flow of goods to the flow of energy, from human mobility to the financial markets. On the international currency markets alone, daily trading volumes average some 3 trillion US dollars. This highlights how, with the aid of digital technology, vast sums of money are being sent around the globe, and they frequently intervene in local economies, with serious social and political repercussions.

The same applies to the material and energy flows, which, for example in the event of war, are then redirected. Technologies not only control individual infrastructures, they also interconnect them. Such networked infrastructures have come to form—alongside the geosphere and the biosphere—a further sphere, namely the technosphere. Linked to the exploitation of nuclear energy and of fossil energies (such as mineral oil, coal, and gas), the technosphere's interventions in the Earth's system have been so profound that scientists have declared a new geological era: the Anthropocene.

These transformations are so far reaching that the fundamental concepts governing our understanding of the world are proving to be inadequate, such as the nature/culture differentiation or the concept

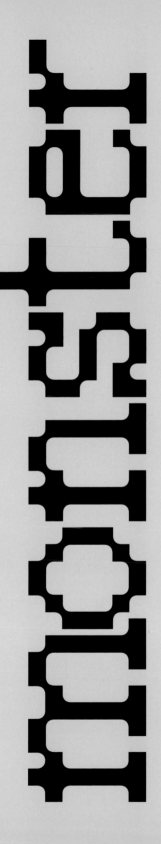

of time. The natural environment we encounter today has been man-
ufactured by humankind. At the same time, we are subject to temporal rhythms in which our planet's deep time is superimposed not only
by normal life cycles, but also by ever-accelerating real-time communications around the globe.

Thanks to digitization, these infrastructures are becoming
increasingly interconnected, prompting the emergence of a complex
technosphere in which technologies, now decoupled from human
agency, are starting to "cooperate" with each other. Thus, increasingly the images from surveillance cameras are being read by other
machines, instead of by human beings. Due to the application of
facial recognition technologies, selection processes are taking place
at rail stations, highways, and so on. And the machine-driven control
of weapons is already a reality in modern warfare.

Consequently, these processes are becoming increasingly
removed from direct human control and responsibility, which now
solely rests with the programming of the machines, into which, as
discussed above, values and power asymmetries are integrated. As
these are determined in the programmers' laboratories, they elude
public scrutiny.

The most cutting-edge developments portending perhaps the
most profound future changes are currently taking place in the field
of artificial intelligence (AI). Here, a stage has already been reached
where, through *deep learning*, machines are now learning from other
machines, or rather machines are advancing their knowledge with the
aid of everyday data. To what extent these learning processes are anal-
ogous to human processes, which they will eventually replace, is still a
matter of academic debate. Whatever the case, Leibniz conferred the
status of monads upon machines—and thus assigned them an autono-
mous role as participating actors in the construction of the world.

Digital culture, in the form of the Internet, has also driven the
rise of English as the universal language. The Internet facilitates
real-time communications across the globe. This has fueled the
emergence of social networks, both in the realm of economics and
in knowledge production, areas where an engagement in permanent
dialogue necessitates a communications medium. Infrastructures
and institutions play a decisive role in the selection of this communications medium—as can be observed in the knowledge sector. In
December 2004, Google collaborated with five leading libraries in

the United States and Great Britain to launch the mammoth Google Book Search Library Project. The goal of the project was to digitize the entire stock of books in these libraries and render them accessible to the world in a database—that is, in the form of a universal library.

Meanwhile, other such digitization projects are now being implemented across the globe, for example in China, where since 1949, some 1.3 million books have been published in Mandarin. The difference is that only speakers of Mandarin have access to these books. Although this represents a vast number of people—Mandarin is the world's most widely spoken language—all bilingual speakers around the world have access to the English texts, which means a universal readership.

Equally decisive, however, are the access criteria and selection mechanisms. The challenge of the digitized universal library is the sheer ever-expanding quantities of texts, which far outstretch a person's ability to access in one lifetime. Consequently, among other things, search engines are required. Accordingly, it is no coincidence that as Google rolled out the Library Project, it simultaneously made available a search engine for accessing this immense quantity of texts.

This circumstance is compounded by the dominance of English-speaking universities and science journals, which stipulate the evaluation standards in the knowledge sector, increasingly requiring authors keen to command international attention to publish in English. This, in turn, acts as an incentive to those hungry for knowledge to at least learn English as a second language.

Although the Internet has accelerated the elevation of English to the lingua franca, it has, at the same time, aided other languages. Languages once suppressed under national linguistic policies are now resurfacing on the Internet. Local and regional tongues, which would be unable to survive in the long term in the classical media, such as books or newspapers, have here found a written medium.

However, the use of most languages remains confined to their respective linguistic communities. For example, languages such as French, German, Hindi, and Japanese are losing significance due to the dominance of English, regressing into merely local phenomena whose untranslatable singularities do not gain access to global discourse.

It is evident that the digital culture cannot be perceived as a particular realm; symbiotic relationships are being forged, one could

even claim that entire ecologies are emerging from these coevolution-
ary processes—as in this case, through the networking of the Internet's knowledge-oriented infrastructures and institutions, with the
natural languages.

As already mentioned, one outcome of these processes is the
hegemony of English as the lingua franca, alongside the establish-
ment of institutions such as search engines and global universities
acting as commercial enterprises. Operating progressively less as
academies or as Leibniz monads of the second order, such institutions objectify knowledge in the form of data, and societal discourse
on the purported indistinguishability of the participating perspectives is suspended.

However, there are also counter-models to the dominance of the
English language. The European Union has enshrined multilingual-
ism within its constitution. As a consequence, the European Court
of Justice maintains its own 2,000-strong department in order to
represent the twenty-four languages of the EU in legal proceedings.
The working language of the judges is French. Due to the principle
of linguistic diversity, a permanent negotiation between different
sets of values, world constructions, and cultural encodings is taking
place. Yet this diversity of perspectives is not only accommodated on
a linguistic level; the perspectives present within the languages are,
in each specific case, being updated by the respective actors and thus
becoming renegotiable—a process that could never be articulated
within the framework of one single hegemonic language.

However, beyond these counter-models to the hegemony of
English, further new structures have been evolving in recent years,
even in the fields of economics and finance. These are aimed at iden-
tifying alternative technologies to replace the commodification of our
experiential and living world, under the hegemonic business models
that have been generated through the concentration of technological
infrastructures in the hands of just a few institutions.

One such alternative is blockchain technology, which operates
with cryptocurrencies, and which formed the foundation for the
introduction of Bitcoin. This digital currency is based on a decentral-
ized public-ledger system. With the aid of a distributed network of
computers, transfers are conducted via the Internet in special peer-
to-peer applications, rendering superfluous a settlement center, such
as a bank. The cryptographic technology ensures that transactions

are only initiated by the respective Bitcoin owners. And it is the inter-action of all the participants, the aggregated individual supply and demand, which determines the value of the currency.

This is to avoid third parties, located beyond the individuals and the community, capitalizing personally on the actions, needs, and interests of the actors, as is the case under digital capitalism. The intention here is to establish a financial technology predicated on cosmological perspectivism. To what extent this technology can deliver on its objective of creating a new societal and individual model, only time will tell. After all, the Internet was also originally launched with the aim of establishing a technology for network-ing individuals to enable their modes of perception and thought to develop across boundaries.

Against the backdrop of an extractive digital capitalism, which is permanently transforming expressions of life into commodities and, in the process, transforming the knowledge society into an "extractive society," the objective must be to regain a diversity of perspectives on both a societal and an individual level—especially in the face of the current realization of just how quickly an extractive capitalism can implode, once the all-decisive consumption fails to materialize. Instead of digital *connectivity*, a community must emerge whose members are all actively participating in the world-creation process. Ultimately, this entails implementing the entire Leibniz program: The alphabet program of the *characteristica universalis* must be comple-mented by the perspective cosmology of the monadology.

Translated from the German by John Rayner

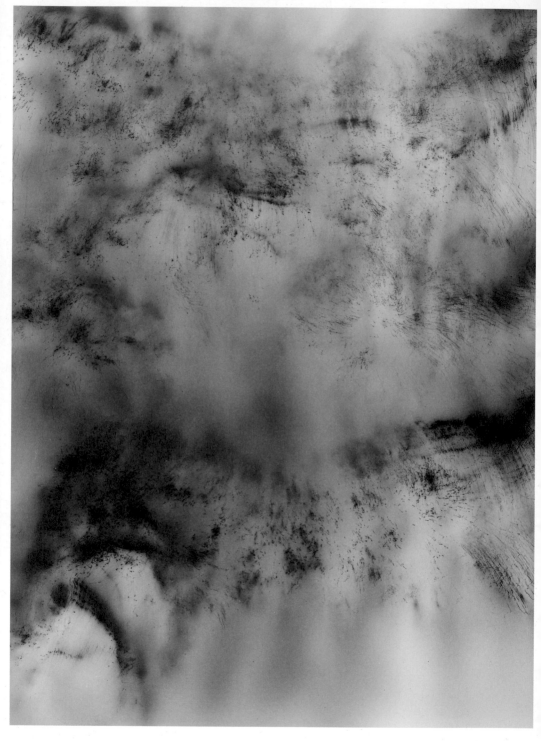

Notes on Writing Systems

I have also loved the alphabet. The letters have colours (as do
numbers) which mingle with the colours of the sounds. I have written poems with this material, and still do. However, I find in myself
no inclination to portray my arbitrary association and familiarity with
this form of writing as venerable or universal. Rather, it seems a pity
that the richness of the world, and of my imagination that echoes it,
found only this poor system to play with. On the other hand, Arte
povera does have a stark beauty, only becoming oppressive when it
sal truth, rather than the random plastic shit it is, ennobled by care
and use.

   To discover the Chinese writing system, then, was, for me as a
writer, like entering a palace or temple of a huge and varied empire.
The organising node of an area so huge that it is a commonplace that
all wisdom must accommodate variety and be extremely humble—
not to "a" "god" but to many. Whatever cultural object one may talk
about, one is sure to find an early Chinese one, and the precedence
will not be clear. These things show either a common origin or the fact
that good ideas may be had by many.

   Maybe using the Chinese system is like using and quoting the
Internet. Not all Truth-truth. You read stuff, you make a sign that
people who know what you are talking about can follow to verify the
details, fact and fiction are mixed, there is no curator, no police. Certain fictions of representation and of bottleneck of dependence do
not arise. The basic atmosphere is: "We all live in this world, look
around." The world is not contained, doubled, or magically represented in the language. There could be some discussion about the
last point, but I am convinced that, just as Buddhism is more of a philosophy than a religion—and seeing how it leaves people free to live
in the world and just is always around to help them think,—language
also is a tool, a beautiful tool, gathering generations of experience
like a good tool does. There is no need to ascribe to it any "more" or
"deeper" sense than the incredible variety and beauty of the work it
does. The idea of representation, so central to Western linguistics,
could be scrapped. Then linguistics might have trouble describing
what European languages are doing, and come to the conclusion that
they may not be quite classifiable as languages, but got stuck somewhere on the way and remained in the dead-end of the alphabet.

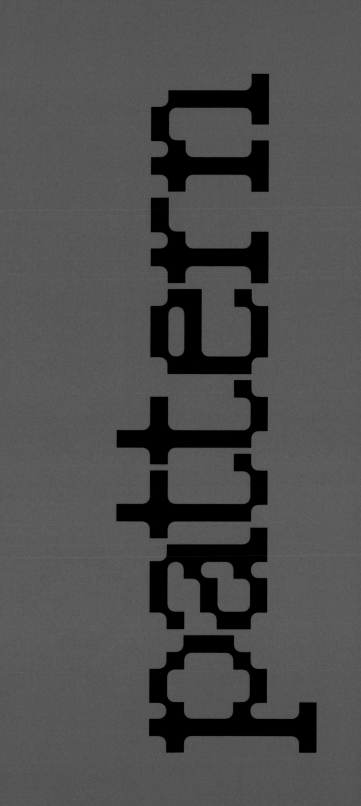

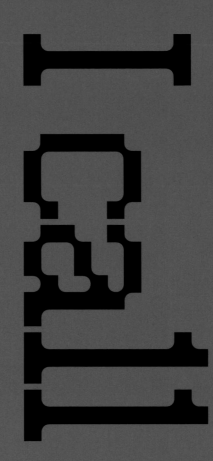

In white people's discussions (painful to read) of the Mi'kmaq language, for example, there is controversy about whether the logographs are an actual writing system or "mere mnemonic devices." Similar discussions surround textile codes and graphic symbols of various peoples. The argument is that a lot of context is necessary to understand the signs. Raising the question: How no-brainer does a writing system have to be to be considered a writing system? A lot of English, btw, is also extremely dependent on context. Try and interpret Graffiti. Cockney Rhyming Slang. Rap.

"Do you have to be able to lie in it for it to be a language?"—There are more tricks in the world than lying.

Of course, it is interesting how the import of other ideas of what to do with language can change a language. It is true that the religions brought writing culture, but it was then often subcultural "misuse" and play with these games that formed new writing cultures. In Korea and Japan, simpler forms of writing were introduced to make it possible for more people to become literate—changing the concept of literacy from a full-time job to something that every human being can use for play and work and spirituality. But remember that general literacy in Europe was only introduced in the eighteenth century. I do not think that any direct causal connection can be made between writing systems and general literacy, which is a problem of the social class structure. Children can learn anything. If the alphabet is more quickly mastered, then you may stop at a lower level of word literacy.

熱い！ 厚い！ 暑い！ Hot (fluid)! Many-layered and thick! Hot (air)! Atsui! Atsui! Atsui! Cummings might agree: "deep is wide." The less units of sense you have, the more sense each one carries. Like the centralisation of France making Paris such a deep or multicultural city. So the huge number of sense units in the Chinese writing system kills the mysticism of the alphabet a little bit. The remarkable thing is that there remains enough depth to ensure each of the signs is still vastly interesting. Spreading it so thin only allows us to realise what a big and deep thing a language is. Or, you could say that it is like planting carrots, if each carrot gets enough space it will fill it up with subtlety.

One could say that the Chinese writing system emphasises or conserves or produces the big difference between written and spoken language. This difference exists in all languages but in phonetic documentation methods, the illusion has come to be cultivated that one simply "catches the spoken word and fixes it on paper," while when writing Chinese, a new playing field is entered. For example, in many cases there are several ideograms one could use to write a word that seems like one in the spoken language and is only differentiated on paper. This goes against the grain of the European linguist who wants to know definitively if it is a homonym or a single word; a verb or a noun just because this pedantic question usually seems quite clear in European writing systems. Only the etymologist churns up the shifts and remixes which have little trace in the phonetic interface—the average speaker can live in the childlike illusion, as in plastic, of a perfect, smooth, eternally contemporary perfection.

Children, learning to write, thus learn to further differentiate words they have learnt as one. Commonsensical and rather unimaginative European and North American commentators including linguists, sociologists, and other foreign experts have often remarked how incredibly cumbersome the ideograph system is. This need not be taken seriously.

The Korean script Hangul is said to be the script that, in the world, represents phonetics most aptly. It was developed by King Sejong in the fifteenth century to help his people learn to read more easily. Its syllabic units consist of parts corresponding to the alphabet's letters. But its aesthetic adheres to the spatial square or rectangular unit.

It is true that the interplay between influences from spoken language and cultures developed in written forms have often tended to refresh languages periodically. The syllabic (phonetic) writing systems in Korean and Japanese came together with fads of intellectual understatement in which the less official medium was used by women and popular writers, developing strong leverage on the classic canon over the years. Different dynamics resulted from the phonetic usage of signs in Chinese and Japanese, the strong erosion by which Japanese developed the Kana syllabic system from phonetically used ideograms, while Hangul is an auctorially designed phonetic system which was introduced by decree. And the unique way in which the syllabary system and the Kanji system are mixed in Japanese excites me in a way only the three-layered, fluidly melodic metre that flows and counter-flows with the sense and grammar in classical Latin verse such as Ovid or Catull could, and which I have always tried to imitate when writing poetry in German.

My experience with the Chinese writing system comes via Japanese. This practice of differentiation, also manifested in the thema-rhema-organisation of the sentence structure, has seemed to me to be a characteristic structural feature of Japanese ways of going about things—as far as I may wager such a generalising observation. There is a sense of *zooming in* through a process of successive differentiation. The Buddhist mystic image of Indra's net also has this feeling of zooming in. While, in the alphabet, one gets the feeling of some kind of basic code completely haphazard—though perhaps it may reinforce a child's illusion of being a little genius, rather than following in the footsteps of others who know more—in the Chinese system it feels like one could go on differentiating forever, until one's collective instruments (of thought) become too blunt. It is a different basic spatial concept of the world, I think. One that agrees better with my experience. But above all, this has been thrilling to me as a proof that there are, in this one real world, several basic metaphorical models. While until then I was chafing at the ropes, protesting against the eurocentric order that seemed to go against the grain of everything I had ever felt, the mere fact of the existence of other forms has turned my attitude of blind, wild protest against the familiar, oppressive and prejudiced world into a thirst to gain the skills of shape-shifting, to remodel my grammatical prejudices, rebuild my world view to accommodate all this, to adapt, to suffer: whatever may be sayable.

Reexploring Kanji Body System

According to 多和田葉子 Yoko Tawada[1] the dictionary is anarchy. And indeed, if you just keep writing from the dictionary, some kind of meaning comes out. 洋要幼用 Yôyôyôyô for example might be understood as "For Childrens' Use As Necessary In The West."

As the human brain tries to make sense of whatever data it is presented with, what happens could be like the zoetrope illusion where a sequence of still images is read by the brain as movement. But while perhaps the stressed language learner experiences a scrambling for sense, the artist 多田佳那子 Kanako Tada rather experiences the language taking over her tongue.

> when you read these poet, kanjis[2] plunder your tongue. They spoke meanings instead of your tongue?—There is more complicated but English like week and weak are same sound, such a play kanji naturally does.—i will show one video—(Tada reads the list of all words read as 「い」 "i" from her electronic dictionary. The 「い」 sounds different depending on the word. It is a long video, maybe 50 kanji or more.)—all kanjis are pronounced 「い」 I realized when I read these kanjis, my sounds is changed. I think I get information from form of kanji, meaning of kanji and figure of 部首 (bushu = radicals).—after I get information, my eyes to deliver order to my tongue how should I pronounce it.—i realized i didn't speak actually, kanji speaks, they borrow my tongue.—opposite thought, if person doesn't know any kanji at least how pronounced it, they just only read so flat.—or kanji's meaning of each—I think it happens all letters. But for example alphabets are very strict of pronounce.—therefore sound play and word play are separate.

1　In Japanese, the surname is generally given first, thus 多和田 is Tawada (and below 多田 Tada).

2　When mentioning the kanji system in foreign languages, sometimes one feels like adding an s for a European plural, sometimes not. Japanese language does not automatically differentiate plural and singular, though there exist disambiguation signals for use when necessary. However, not pluralizing foreign words can give an exoticizing touch in the English. There is also the issue of deciding on "the" or "a," which can feel totally unnecessary to speakers of many languages such as Slavic languages, Chinese or Japanese. The more I realize this, the a / the distinction at times to me also feels as unnecessary as wearing a bra.

umm I also tangle my brain as well ~~

Yoko san said Japanese politician use divinely katakana and kanji to manipulate people. For example, at the press conference on the 12th of March 2011, politicians used a combination of the foreign word written in katakana メルトダウン (merutodaun) with the unusual 4-kanji expression 炉心溶融 (roshinyôyû) to designate the new clear meltdown. four-kanji expression it makes a stable feeling. Both were new words. no images and no connection to Hiroshima and Nagasaki bombings.[3]

Alphabet is very strict to pronounce so maybe this rule put away to speakers emotion or uniqueness?

I wonder japanese, korean or some countries import alphabet words a lot. Turkey and Vietnam even use alphabet to write.

and katakana, alphabet are used in daily life chat. But in alphabet world it never happened? Only tatoo or hip star t-shirts??— maybe like blockchain technology.

i see.

yes, only tattoos.

Occidental import food and art and philosophy from orient But nowadays what is more provocative is that they are hiding that they stole.

pride based on nothing, ne.

未だ大泥棒が偉い時代 (Now is still the era of large scale theft).

---

3   多和田葉子、言葉と歩く日記、東京、岩波、2013年 (Tawada, Yoko, *Diary of walking with words*, Tokyo: Iwanami 2013), pp. 131-32.

p. 4 bauhaushaus 家出

甘いと、尼さんです。It's "sweet," and "nun." The color is 朱色, Japanese vermillion red. Shuiro. I was thinking of them being teenagers at the Bauhaus family, leaving home in protest.

p. 14 Valleygirl 只只只

Shikaku (square) – 詩客 Shi kaku (a poet) – 資格 shikaku (qualification, capacity) – 然く shika+ku（in the way indicated, in such a condition or manner[†])[4] – 鹿食う Shika kuu (eat a deer) – 丸々 Maru maru (circle circle, roly-poly, completely, wholly, chubby) – 参る mairu (visit = respect word) – 円 en (circle) – 。period (maru) – ぱです。-ppa desu. (sounds like: being Europe or being popcorn-like)
三角 Sankaku (triangle) – 参格 sankaku (qualification of participation) – 産岳 sangaku (i was given birth hill) – 氵 sanzui (droplets of water) – 酸 san (acid carbonate) – 再入荷 sainyûka (merchandise delivered again because it is popular) – 最終 saishû (finally) – 参加者食う sankasha kû (eat participants) – 採集 saishû (collect bugs) – 歳集 saishû (gathering age) – 待つ Matsu (waiting) – 松 matsu (pine tree) – 末 matsu (at the end) – 度 do (degree) – 土 do (soil) – 奴 do, yatsu (a guy) – 努度 (effort degree*) – 怒度 (angry degree*!!) – 足 dô (foot) – do (1st note in the Solfeggio system) – 土曜 dô yô (Saturday) – 何処 doko (where) – 土語 dogo (local language) – 誰 dare? (who are you?)
In green, diagonally: 只只只 Tada tada tada... meaning only only only, but but but—or of course yours truly. Since we talked about valley girls and high rising terminals, you know. That way of leaving anything you say hanging in space like a kind of question?

p. 55 Kanji-gyaggu

尼 ama (nun/female diver) – 海女 ama (female diver) – 甘 ama (sweet) – amah (nanny) – 安摩 ama (a relaxing rub) – アマ ama (amateur) – 亜麻 ama (flax) – 雨 ame/ama (rain) – 天 ama (the sky and the heaven) – 故意 koi (on purpose) – 虎威 koi (the ability of a tiger to impress other animals/military power) – 恋 koi (romance) – coy – 来い (koi!) come (to order) – 濃い? koi? is this deep or dark? – coin – 乞い/請い koi (beg/ask to help) – koi – 鯉 koi (koi) – 胡渭 Ko I (name in Japanese of a Chinese scholar who lived around 1800) – c/o, i – Collie – コイ Koi Yo! – 洋 yô (western) – 要 yô (important) – 用 yô (something have to do) – 孕 yô (pregnant) – 益 yô (profit) – 良う you (be good) – 酔う you (be drunkun) – 影 ei (shadow) – 様 yô (style, like this) – 拗 yô (jealous) – 永 ei (forever) – よう yô (hey)
I have been reading the anthropologist Cho Han Haejoang recently, who started out doing research on female pearl divers. That is amah. But if you find woman to bring up kids, that is also amah.

---

4 † marks words no longer in use, * marks neologisms coined by Tada.

尼 海女 甘 amah 安摩アマ

亜麻 雨 天

故意 虚侮 恋、coy 来い 濃い？

coin 匂い／請い koi 鯉

胡渭 cloy collie コイ
Humei

ヒ良 洋要用 孕益良う 酔う影ゝ

様、掬永よう

On the Cosmotechnical Nature of Writing[1]

Apropos of the New Alphabet

In January 2019, the Haus der Kulturen der Welt introduced a new long-term program titled *The New Alphabet*, referring to the new form of writing brought about by digital technologies. Digital writing is more likely to be systemic than all precedent forms of writing. Systemic not only in the sense of being coherent, but also in the sense that all writing which follows, based on this medium, is essentially calculable. The *digital* now becomes the substrate of all writing, while formerly the latter was considered the substrate of language—in the literal sense of the term, meaning that which underlies. What is the significance of this New Alphabet? It is no longer only a form of representation operating on the general linguistic level, but also one which enables multiple algorithms to expand across different functions, from knowledge representation to translation and decision-making, and which extends from the linguistic domain directly into other domains, including education, the legal and commercial sectors, and so on.

Certainly, many sociological and anthropological studies are already underway; but here I would like to approach the issue from a different perspective. Digitalization means precisely unification and synchronization. The New Alphabet implies not only a medium of writing, but also more importantly the realization of an extensible and unifiable technical system mediated by data. It was the continued desire to explore the fundamental question of metaphysics that culminated in the thinking of Leibniz and later Hegel and which was realized in cybernetic theory. Both philosophers triumphed in different ways but with interesting intersections, which will be visited later. For the New Alphabet, the digital is fundamentally a question of a system, in connection with, but also far beyond, the same notion that was central to eighteenth-century European philosophy. Therefore, I would like to apprehend this question from both the histories

---

1   An earlier version of this essay (with a different focus) was published as "Writing and Cosmotechnics", *Derrida Today*, vol. 13, no. 1 (May 2020), pp. 17–32.

of philosophy and technology. However, first, it is important to point out that the digital is not simply binary code, on the contrary, the binary—as often attributed to Leibniz and the Chinese divination system of the *I Ching*—is only one reductive representation of the digital. In my own vocabulary, the binary is only one *order of magnitude* of the digital. Let me begin by taking the document I am currently typing: I could start by decomposing it, into characters, then ASCII codes, and further into binary codes of 0 and 1; then below 0 and 1 are the representations of its signals evident in electronic devices such as transistors; and further beneath are the activities of electrons. Above the binaries are other different layers, notably the recursive algorithms, which perform grammatical checks and the comparisons of versions, and so on. The concept of *recursivity* was already present in Leibniz's concept of the monad, which constantly reflects the reflections of other monads containing the whole world from its viewpoint. Yet the concept might be even more profoundly evident in Hegel's logic, which according to Gotthard Günther already anticipated the feedback system of cybernetics.[2] In other words, the binary is only one magnitude. Therefore, reducing our understanding of the New Alphabet to the binary may prevent us from understanding its significance and its impacts, which is why it is essential to apprehend the New Alphabet from a much broader historical and technological context.

I attempted to broach the question of the digital in my two treatises *On the Existence of Digital Objects* (2016) and *Recursivity and Contingency* (2019).[3] The former tackles the question of representation or ontology in and of computation, while the latter deals with recursive algorithms, charting a history of recursivity from Leibniz to cybernetics. In this essay, I would like to take a different direction by articulating it in relation to what I call cosmotechnics.[4] The concept of cosmotechnics questions and challenges the conventional

2   Gotthard Günther, "Seele und Maschine," in *Beiträge zur Grundlegung einer operationsfähigen Dialektik, Vol. 1*. Hamburg: Felix Meiner Verlag, 1976, pp. 75–90, here p. 85.

3   Yuk Hui, *On the Existence of Digital Objects*. Minneapolis, MN: University of Minnesota Press, 2016; Yuk Hui, *Recursivity and Contingency*. London: Rowman and Littlefield International, 2019.

4   Yuk Hui, *The Question Concerning Technology in China: An Essay in Cosmotechnics*. Falmouth: Urbanomic, 2019 [2016].

understanding of technology as being anthropologically and functionally universal (i.e. an extension of organs, an externalization of memory) and that there is a single history of technological evolution; it suggests that, instead of understanding technology as neutral and universal, we must expose the multiplicity of cosmotechnics within different cultures and throughout history, which we call *technodiversity*. Such diversity is not only expressed in different artifacts, but more significantly, it is represented in different systems of knowledge and in the rich but nuanced relations between humans and their milieus.

The questioning into the essence of technology, either in terms of *poiesis* for the Greeks or *Gestell* for the moderns,[5] such as Martin Heidegger and many others in the West have done, often misses the concept of technodiversity and therefore it risks imposing a European Prometheanism onto other cultures (though this might happen unconsciously). With this essay titled "On the Cosmotechnical Nature of Writing," the intention is to expose some of the fundamental differences between phonetic and non-phonetic, alphabetic and non-alphabetic writing in order to reflect on the New Alphabet. If we conceive the New Alphabet as a unifying and synchronizing system, we may want to raise a seemingly distant question: *Will digital writing eliminate the diversity of previous forms of writing because digital technology today is the medium of synchronization?* One may immediately argue that when one writes in Chinese with a computer, one still uses Chinese characters and, therefore, there is not really a hegemonic synchronization, for the New Alphabet only provides a neutral foundation. Yet, the basis of this objection still rests on a dualistic way of understanding the relation between culture and technology, and mistakenly assumes that culture can remain intact when it adopts a different set of technologies. However, in order to elucidate this

---

5   According to Heidegger, the Greek term *technē* means "bringing forth" (*Hervorbringen*), whose function was the unconcealment of Being, understood as truth (*A-letheia*); the essence of modern technology is enframing (*Gestell*), meaning that it treats all beings as standing reserves, or resources, with its mode of unconcealment challenging and violent, see Martin Heidegger, "The Question Concerning Technology," in *The Question Concerning Technology and Other Essays*, trans. William Lovitt. New York: Harper and Row, 1977, pp. 3–35.

point, it is necessary to take a detour through the history of philosophy—or more precisely the episode concerning deconstruction, often associated with the French philosopher Jacques Derrida. The reason for this is that it exposes the limit of the concept of writing (but also *technics* in general) in European thought, and witnesses a historical debate concerning technodiversity that the remainder of this essay will examine.

Phonogram versus
Pictogram

The philosophical debate initiated by deconstruction concerns the question of writing. It is this philosophical and historical investigation of writing, that human beings have been practicing since the beginning of history, which suspends—or *epechein* in phenomenology—the naïve view of writing as simply one form of expression among many others. And through the notion of writing, Jacques Derrida deconstructs the history of metaphysics. To understand Derrida's thesis, but more importantly to investigate a task that Derrida invoked but didn't pursue further after writing *Of Grammatology*, we will have to briefly discuss his concept of writing. Writing has to be understood primarily as traces, or more precisely as supplement to memory. To put it briefly and probably over-simplistically: technics is the support that enables the game between protention and retention (in the sense of Edmund Husserl) and it is also this "retention and protention of differences, spacing and temporalizing, a play of traces" that gives us the concept of *différance* and archi-writing.[6] Likewise, in *Of Grammatology*, Derrida opened up the question of *technodiversity*, but he didn't elaborate on it. His discourse on technodiversity centers on the difference between European phonetic writing and Chinese pictorial writing. In sinology, some have referred to Chinese writing as having the form of an ideogram. In this essay, I contest this, because I do not think that the question of form, of *eidos,* is central to Chinese writing, as Derrida understood as well.

---

6   Jacques Derrida, "Différance" [1968], in Julie Rivkin and Michael Ryan (eds), *Literary Theory: An Anthology*. Oxford: Blackwell Publishing, 2004, pp. 278–99, here p. 289.

Derrida begins *Of Grammatology* with a rather intriguing statement: "the notion of technics can *never* simply clarify the notion of writing."[7] He explains, "I believe on the contrary that a certain sort of question about the meaning and origin of writing precedes, or at least merges with, a certain type of question about the meaning and origin of technics."[8] What does Derrida want to suggest here? Is there a *temporal* discrepancy between the origin of writing and the origin of technics? Could we interpret this as saying that writing can *never* be reduced to a general or universal understanding of technics as the supplement?[9]

The difference between Western phonetic writing and Chinese pictorial writing has been articulated for centuries. And according to Derrida's reading, the European conception of Chinese writing could be divided into two attitudes which would be either the "hyperbolic admiration" incarnated in Leibniz or the "ethnocentric scorn" exemplified by Hegel.[10] *Of Grammatology* has lengthy expositions dedicated to elaborating on the differences between Leibniz and Hegel, which one could read, I argue, as an exploration of the cosmotechnical thinking of the East and the West. We know that Leibniz admired Chinese writing, because not only did the hexagrams of the *I Ching* resemble the binary system that he had developed earlier, but also because it seemed to him a somewhat developed system based on visual symbols. The Chinese had used a limited number of visual symbols in order to create a language that had a high capacity of expression, akin to what Leibniz aspired to in his "the best of all possible worlds":

7   Jacques Derrida, *De la grammatologie*. Paris: Gallimard, 1967; trans. Gayatri Chakravorty Spivak, *Of Grammatology*. Baltimore, MD, and London: Johns Hopkins University Press (corrected edition), 1998, p. 8, italics the author's.

8   Ibid.

9   If we understand from Derrida's 1968 essay "Différance," published a year after *Of Grammatology,* that archi-writing—the retention and protention of differences—is technical in nature, then we can conclude that archi-writing (an economy of the supplement made possible by technical traces) comes prior to writing. However, it seems to me that such an understanding is not sufficient in the *Of Grammatology* context where Derrida opened a significant inquiry into diversity, which he failed to pursue further later in his writing.

10   Derrida, *Of Grammatology*, p. 87.

God has chosen the most perfect world, that is, the one which
is at the same time the simplest in hypotheses and the richest
in phenomena, as might be a line in geometry whose construction is easy and whose properties and effects are extremely
remarkable and widespread.[11]

Chinese writing confirms Leibniz's optimism: In it, it is possible to
find symbols and rules of combination that should allow a perfect
and global language to appear. Chinese writing remains an inspira-
tion for Leibniz's creation of a *characteristica universalis*. It should
be noted that *characteristica universalis* is considered the philosophical foundation of today's digital writing and that Norbert Wiener
considered Leibniz as the patron saint of cybernetics. However, there
is no simple, linear relationship between Chinese writing, universal
characters, and digital writing. Rather, as will become clearer, the
complexities (in both technological and political senses) have yet to
be evaluated. The universal character is universal in the sense that it
is visual and therefore it may be able to bypass phonetic differences:

Those who know the Chinese characters are right to believe
that it will become a universal character, whose written form
would be understood by all the world. If all peoples in the
world could agree on the designation of a thing by a character,
one people could pronounce it differently from the other. And
we could introduce a Universal Symbolism.[12]

11	Gottfried Wilhelm von Leibniz, *Discourse on Metaphysics and Other
	Essays: On the Ultimate Origination of Things*, trans. Daniel Garber and
	Roger Ariew. Indianapolis, IN: Hackett Publishing, 1989, p. 39.
12	Gottfried Wilhelm von Leibniz, *New Essays on Human Understanding*,
	trans. and ed. Peter Remnant and Jonathan Bennett. Cambridge:
	Cambridge University Press, 1981, p. 290.

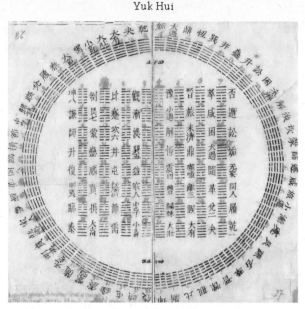

I Ching, 64 hexagrams based on a binary code.

Substance versus Relation

Hegel reproached Leibniz by saying that the Chinese written language is imperfect because there is no correspondence between the written and the spoken; and indeed, it is an obstacle to science. The German language is superior and easier to learn since it only employs twenty-six letters; on the contrary, "the Chinese do not have twenty-six letters, but instead many thousands of characters (*Zeichen*). The number of them necessary for ordinary purposes is 9,351, and in the opinion of some more than 10,000; scholars need 80,000-90,000."[13] Against this, Hegel claims: "It is only to the exegeticism of Chinese spiritual culture that their hieroglyphic writing is suited." That is, the "analytic notation of representations [...] which seduced Leibniz to the point of wrongly preferring this script to the alphabetic, rather contradicts the

13   G. W. F. Hegel, *Lectures on the Philosophy of World History, Vol. 1: Manuscripts of the Introduction and the Lectures of 1822-3,* ed. and trans. Robert F. Brown and Peter C. Hodgson. Oxford: Oxford University Press, 2011, pp. 239-40.

fundamental exigency of language in general, namely the noun."[14] How might we understand Hegel's fierce comment? Derrida explains that by "noun," Hegel means substantiality, the other name of presence and of *ousia* (often translated as essence). According to Plato's theory of forms and ideas, the ideal form (*eidos*) behind all empirical appearance of a particular being is its essence. Aristotle's *Metaphysics* (Book Z) proffers three candidates for *ousia*: 1) matter, 2) form, and 3) a compound of form and matter; Aristotle gave form (*eidos*) alone the name of *ousia*.[15] It is for this reason that I object to the reference of Chinese characters as ideograms, since it is inaccurate to think of an *idea* in the Greek sense. I prefer the term "pictogram", since Chinese characters are oriented less to the ideal form of being and more to their relation among beings. In this respect, Hegel is still grounded within Western metaphysics, in an onto-theology opened by Plato and Aristotle, while Leibniz, partially with the influence of the Jesuits in China, especially Father Bouvet, has attempted to go beyond such a view.

We can at least claim that in *Of Grammatology*, Derrida provided a synthesis for readers to understand these two "technical facts" of Chinese and Western characters philosophically. It is true that both written forms could be thought of as supplements, as exteriorized memory, and that there is a mechanism of archi-writing at play in terms of different orders of retention and protention. However, there are significant differences that are probably "prior to" (if not coincident with) the origin of technics. These differences are fundamental and irreducible to the technical mediums of expression. The Chinese also had cave paintings (as in the West). However, they developed a form of writing informed by a different cosmology and a different philosophical temperament. With this in mind, we may want to reconsider Derrida's strategy of opposing substance and relation, and their incarnations in phonetic writing and pictorial writing. Substance and relation are two categories full of tension within the history of Western philosophy. In Aristotle's *Categories*, we know that relation is considered one of the nine accidents of substance (subject); however, by the end of his section on the "relative" in *Categories*, Aristotle left the interpretation open-ended:

14   Derrida, *Of Grammatology*, pp. 25–26.
15   Aristotle, *Metaphysics*, ed. and trans. John Marrington. London: Everyman's Library, 1956, Book Z, 1028b4.

Indeed, if our definition of that which is relative was complete, it is very difficult, if not impossible, to prove that no substance is relative. If however, our definition was not complete, if those things are only properly called relative in the case of which relation to an external object is a necessary condition of existence, perhaps some explanation of the dilemma may be found.[16]

The question of the nature of the relative and the relationship between relative and substance concerned almost every medieval philosopher at the time: Avicenna, Thomas Aquinas, Albert the Great, Henry of Ghent, Duns Scotus, to name but a few. This is largely because it is closely related to the Trinitarian question, namely, to explain "how in God the persons are identical with the divine essence, yet different among themselves."[17] Even though the concern of various interpretations was largely theological, their philosophical speculations should not be overlooked, for example: (1) Is substance relative at all? (2) Is relation a real (extramental) being? For the purposes of this essay, it should be pointed out that substance and relation remain two irreconcilable concepts in Western philosophy. These concepts continue to be contradictory until the more recent emergence of a philosophy of relation, exemplified in the work of Alfred North Whitehead. The fraught relationship between substance and relation brings us to the distinction between synchronization and heterogeneity. Derrida claims with regard to Hegel's phonocentric proposal for the "*Aufhebung* [sublation] of other writings, particularly of hieroglyphic scripts and the Leibnizian characteristics"[18] that "non-phonetic writing breaks the noun apart." Then Derrida continues, "It describes relations and not appellations [...] in this regard Leibniz is as disturbing as the Chinese in Europe."[19]

Today, in the digital age, with Leibniz no longer among us, the Chinese may become even more disturbing: digitization in China has

16   Aristotle, "Categories," in J. Barnes (ed.), *The Complete Works of Aristotle*. Princeton, NJ: Princeton University Press, 1991, 8a28–34.
17   Jos Decorte, "Relatio as Modus Essendi: The Origins of Henry of Ghent's Definition of Relation," *International Journal of Philosophical Studies*, vol. 10, no. 3 (2002), pp. 309–36, here p. 309.
18   Derrida, *Of Grammatology*, p. 25.
19   Ibid., p. 26.

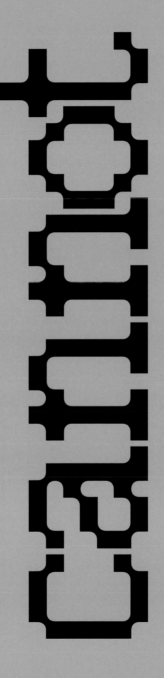

like water

taken up a much faster pace than elsewhere in the world. We are in an age of global technological competition tending towards technological singularity and superintelligence. Digital technology is the medium of synchronization, and one is justified to doubt if this synchronization could really open up a diachronization, or whether it would only introduce a limited heterogeneity within a highly homogenized system (in the same way that multiculturalism has been contained within a secular and modernized society). Derrida hinted at the tension between substantial thinking and a thinking based on relations, but did not enter into the question of relation here, since this is a thinking different from the Western tradition, which is why Heidegger renounced the development of a theory of relation in §18 of *Sein und Zeit* after his analysis of the ready-to-hand.[20] We must put this right: it is not that there is no relationality in alphabetic writing. The composition of a word can be analyzed according to relations such as vowels and consonants, prefix and postfix, subject and predicates in the sentence. This is why Bertrand Russell in *The Principle of Mathematics* criticized Aristotelian logic based on subject and predicates, arguing instead for a calculus of relation and *relata*.[21] So what is the question of relation that Derrida hinted at but did not explore? Leibniz hypothesized that Chinese writing started with the hexagram and evolved into the pictogram. This may be questionable when the history of writing in China is studied with some degree of care, but Leibniz's claim that both hexagram and pictogram come from the observation of phenomenon and pattern is also not without reason. In one of the *I Ching*'s most important commentaries, *Xi Ci*, we read:

> Anciently, when Bao-xi had come to the rule of all under Heaven, looking up, he contemplated the brilliant phenomenon exhibited in the sky, and looking down he surveyed the patterns shown on the earth. He contemplated the ornamental appearances of birds and beasts and the (different) suitabilities of the soil. Near at hand, in his own person, he found things for consideration, and the same at a distance, in things in general. On this he devised the eight trigrams, to show fully the

20   Martin Heidegger, *Sein und Zeit*. Tübingen: Max Niemeyer, 2006.
21   See Hui, *On the Existence of Digital Objects*, Chapter 3.

attributes of the spirit-like and intelligent (operations working secretly), and to classify the qualities of the myriads of things.[22]

Writing is a visual abstraction of the movement or change of phenomenon, which is called *xiang* (象); it means, elephant, phenomenon, but also image. Chinese writing is a philosophy of things, as the famous Bishop of Chester, John Wilkins, says. The basic construction of Chinese writing is pictograms, but not all Chinese characters are drawings of patterns and phenomena, since other techniques are also in use to construct characters[23] However, pictograms remain the basic model, and famously the Tang art historian Zhang Yanyuan (c. 815–875) claims that painting and writing come from the same source in China.[24]

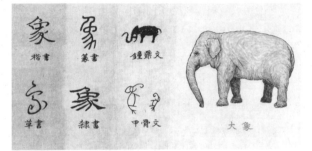

The evolution of the character 象 meaning both elephant and phenomenon/image.

22   See *Xi Ci* II, trans. James Legge, http://ctext.org/book-of-changes/ xi-ci-xia/ens (2006–2020). I have slightly modified Legge's translation: "What appears in the heaven as phenomenon, takes concrete form/ pattern on the earth (在天成象，在地成形)."

23   These techniques, known as the six types of writing based on how they are formed or derived, include pictographs (象形; *xiàngxíng*), ideographic (指事; *zhǐshì*), compound ideographs (會意; *huìyì*), phono-semantic compounds (形聲; *xíngshēng*), rebus or phonetic loan characters (假借; *jiǎjiè*), and derivative cognates (轉注; *zhuǎn zhù*).

24   See Zhang Yanyuan, "Notes on Famous Paintings of the Past Dynasties," in *A Complete Collection of Chinese Calligraphy and Painting, vol. 1.* Shanghai: Shanghai Calligraphy and Painting Publication House, 1993.

Concerning the question of pattern, we can read a critique of substantialism that the cybernetician Gregory Bateson articulated. In *Steps to an Ecology of Mind,* when commenting on Alfred Korzybski's famous dictum that "the map is not the territory," Bateson argued that Western thinking is essentially a thinking of substance that ignores the question of pattern:

> [H]is statement came out of a very wide range of philosophic thinking, going back to Greece, and wriggling through the history of European thought over the last 2000 years. In this history, there has been a sort of rough dichotomy and often deep controversy. There has been a violent enmity and bloodshed. It all starts, I suppose with the Pythagoreans versus their predecessors, and the argument took the shape of 'Do you ask what it's made of—earth, fire, water, etc.?' Or do you ask, 'What is its pattern?' Pythagoras stood for inquiry into pattern rather than inquiry into substance.[25]

Like deconstruction, cybernetics in the 20th century is also an intellectual movement that wants to move away from a substantialism into a process characterized by feedback and recursive operations.

In contrast to the anti-substantialist thinking proposed by Derrida among others, I have been attempting to construct a philosophy of relation since my first book *On the Existence of Digital Objects*, a study of relational thinking in and beyond the digital. Here I argue that writing is not simply an abstraction of meaning that embeds logical relations (which I call discursive relations, namely that which could be articulated by language); it also embeds what I call existential relations, meaning the relation between humans and the external world. From this view, we see how the unified meaning of a character can be decomposed into parts with different meanings, which are the relations and significations being observed in the world and the cosmos. For example, if we look at the character that means legal or law (法): On the left, we have water; on the right, we have the symbol of "go." Law means precisely letting flow like water. Another

25   Gregory Bateson, *Steps to an Ecology of Mind: Collected Essays in Anthropology, Psychiatry, Evolution, and Epistemology.* Chicago, IL: University of Chicago Press, 2000, p. 455.

character, to rest (休), is a human next to a tree; the tree–human relation constitutes rest.

Assuming that the above interpretation is clear, we come to understand what Derrida is saying in the quote at the beginning of this essay: "the notion of technics can *never* simply clarify the notion of writing." This needs to be understood in a sense that is probably different from what Derrida himself wanted to say—at least it is beyond the concept of the supplement. We see that Chinese writing as a practice of traces embeds already-rich relations and patterns that could not be identified in phonetic writing. This relational type of composition embeds an original way of describing humans and the cosmos. To write is not simply to deliver communicative meaning, but also to ponder upon the relation between humanity and the cosmos. Of course, these uncanny relations conceal themselves when one develops the habitude of writing, so that the mind alone becomes the subject of enunciation and exteriorization; however, it is also by mastering writing as an art form, instead of a mere means of communication, that one understands the relation between writing and the Dao. In his classic work, *The Literary Mind and the Carving of Dragons*, the sixth-century literary scholar Liu Xie states: "The Dao inspires writing and writing illuminates the Dao."[26] In ancient China, to say that someone could write did not mean the same as it does today—writing or typing an article—rather, it meant that someone practiced calligraphy. To become a writer was also to be a calligrapher, to have mastered the art of writing, to give spirit to the pictogram, also to search for the Dao through writing.

After the New Alphabet

Of course, as we no longer live in ancient times, and modernization has rendered such traditions obsolete, any homecoming is difficult if not dangerous. The spirit of *Dao* was displaced by modern astrophysics, and since has fled in the face of Elon Musk's SpaceX Dragon spacecraft. With digital writing, everything could be reduced to twenty-six alphabets, which could be further reduced to ASCII code

26   See Liu Xie, *The Literary Mind and the Carving of Dragons*, trans. Vincent Yu-chung Shih. Hong Kong: The Chinese University Press, 1983.

and then to binary code; yet there are different ways of reduction, just as there are different input methods. Without delving too far back into the history of Chinese typewriters, and without listing all the input methods, showing two major input methods will suffice, one used in Taiwan and Hong Kong (traditional Chinese) and the other in Mainland China (simplified Chinese, implemented since 1955). The first of these was named after the inventor of Cangjie, a form of writing based on the composition of pictograms; the character law (法), for example, can be decomposed into three symbols. The second form is based on romanization, which is called Pinyin today.

水土戈

| 1 法 | 2 溘 | 3 滧 | 4 潙 | 5 水土戈 | 6 egi |

fa

1 法	2 发	3 罚	4 伐	5 乏	6 😂
阀	珐	発	髮	筏	砝
垡	發	廢	撥	髮	罰
贬	閥	汎	琺	醗	茷
疢	蘍	廗	汲	妦	栰
茷	罭	橃	茷	紣	瀆
Fréquence	Radical	Trait	Emoji	Structure

Screen captures made by the author.

The romanization of Chinese writing was a project instigated at the beginning of the twentieth century, which proposed to completely abandon hieroglyphic writing and adopt alphabetic writing instead. Fortunately, the hieroglyph has not been abandoned completely, because, at the same time, the project of Pinyin (using twenty-six alphabets as phonetic annotation of Chinese characters) is almost complete. It is time to pause with a question: What is the point of coming back to the question of Chinese writing and the differences with it and phonetic writing if all of them could be typed out alphabetically? The aim is not to oppose the digital and the analogue, the West and the East; rather, the point is to take a step back to ask whether there are different histories of technologies and, if so, to ask what the relations between these technologies, humans, and the cosmos are. With writing as an example, I have tried to show that it is not possible to identify and compare phonetic writing and non-phonetic writing in a narrow sense, namely the exteriorization of sound and the practice of making traces. Writing here is also a metaphor, that is, it is not reducible to a technique or a general concept of technics, but is rather what situates technics within a cosmic reality in the same manner that a ground relates to a figure in Gestalt psychology. The ground stabilizes the figure while the figure also transforms the ground. However, when it produces a subversion of figure and ground, then we arrive at what Gilles Deleuze calls a transcendental stupidity, which brings us to the very danger we are facing.

If the New Alphabet, as I have presented it, denotes a totalizing and unifying system then, in response, I propose a fragmentation, not only of the system, but also of the definite future ahead of us. Fragmentation here means to conceive of a multiplicity of technologies, or cosmotechnics. This diversity should be recognized beyond the European history of epistemology and technology. This inquiry cannot stop here as there are still too many unresolved questions: How should the question of technodiversity be raised when intellectuals are still craving an artificial general intelligence (AGI)? We must return to history in order to orientate ourselves where we stand, but also to create a sense of distance. Will it be possible to find strategies that liberate us from this apocalyptic end of technological singularity and reopen the question of the future? Discussion about the New Alphabet should critically engage these questions without losing sight because of the fantasy of technological acceleration.

Clearly, I fall far from the mark in answering this question in such a short essay. This *Umwertung*, or revaluation of the concept of technology—that is to say deviation from a conventional understanding of a lineage from the Greek *technē* to modern technology—is a shock; and this shock is also a suspension, which may allow us to look at modern technology anew and negotiate a new relation with it. By "negotiate a new relation," I do not only mean putting technology to a different use, but also to design tools that embed sets of relations and epistemologies that are different from those that currently dominate, which come mostly from Silicon Valley. To return to histories of technologies is not to constrain modern technology with culture, or to set up a dichotomy between them, but rather to reconcile culture and technics in the sense of Gilbert Simondon.[27] The ultimate question to invoke here is: Will it be possible to conceive technodiversities by reappropriating the New Alphabet? Reappropriation in the sense of not being simply determined by technology, but transforming it in order to give it new direction. We may want to call this reappropriation *Ereignis* in the Martin Heidegger sense, a transformative act, which *reframes* the *enframing* (*Gestell*) of modern technology. And it is in this attempt at questioning that we respond to the *aporia* of synchronicity, which we raised at the beginning of this essay, in order to conceive a true futurism made possible by technodiversity.

27   See Gilbert Simondon, *On the Mode of Existence of Technical Objects*. Minneapolis, MN: Univocal, 2017.

From
THE HATRED OF POETRY

I remember speaking a word whose meaning I didn't know but about which I had some inkling, some intuition, then inserting that word into a sentence, testing how it seemed to fit or chafe against the context and the syntax, rolling the word around, as it were, on my tongue. I remember my feeling that I possessed only part of the meaning of the word, like one of those fragmented friendship necklaces, and I had to find the other half in the social world of speech. I remember walking around as a child repeating a word I'd overheard, applying it wildly, and watching how, miraculously, I was rarely exactly wrong. If you are five and you point to a sycamore or an idle backhoe or a neighbor stooped over his garden or to images of these things on a television set and utter "vanish" or utter "varnish" you will never be only incorrect; if your parent or guardian   Vanish or varnish is curious she can find a meaning that makes you almost eerily prescient—the neighbor is dying, losing weight, or the backhoe has helped a structure disappear or is glazed in rainwater or the sheen of spectacle lends to whatever appears on-screen a strange finish. To derive your understanding of a word by watching others adjust to your use of it: Do you remember the feeling that sense was provisional and that two people could build around an utterance a world in which any usage signified? I think that's poetry. And when I felt I finally mastered a word, when I could slide it into a sentence with a satisfying click, that wasn't poetry anymore—that was something else, something functional within a world, not the liquefaction of its limits.

Remember how easily our games could breakdown or reform or redescribe reality? The magical procedure was always first and foremost repetition: every kid knows the phenomenon that psychologists call "semantic saturation," wherein a word is repeated until it feels emptied of sense and becomes mere sound; "to repeat, monotonously, some common word, until the sound, by dint of frequent repetition, ceased to convey any idea whatever to the mind," as Poe describes it in the story "Berenice." Your parents enforce a bedtime and, confined to your bed, you yell "bedtime" over and over again until whatever meaning seemed to dwell therein is banished along with all symbolic order and you're a little feral animal underneath the glowing plastic stars. Linguistic repetition, you learn from an early age, can give form or take it away because it forces a confrontation with the malleability of language and the world we build with it, build upon it. Most horrifying was to do this or have it done to your own name, worst of all by some phalanx of chanting kids on the playground—to be reminded how easily you could be expelled from the human community, little innominate snot-nosed feral animal too upset even to tattle. And what would you say? "They broke my name." The teacher would just instruct you to cast a weak spell back: "Sticks and stones may break my bones, but words ...."

That's my name; don't wear it out.

We call these children's games, not children's work, but isn't a child precisely one who doesn't yet observe a clear distinction between what counts as labor and what counts as leisure? All children are poets in that sense. I'm asking you to locate your memory of that early linguistic instability, of language as a creative and destructive force. I have done the reading and the reading suggests that we always experience this power as withdrawing from us or we from it—if we didn't distance from this capacity it would signal our failure to be assimilated into the actual, adult world, i.e. we would be crazy. Our resentment of that falling away from poetry takes the form (among other forms) of contempt for grown-up poets and for poems; poets, who, by their very nature, accuse us of that distance, make it felt, but fail to close it.

I remember when the Hypermarket opened in Topeka, a 235,000-square-foot big-box store with vast and towering aisles of brightly lit, brightly packaged goods, remember the cereal aisle in particular, "family sized" boxes of Cap'n Crunch repeating as far as the eye could see. And roller skating—I'm not kidding— among these sugary infinities were young uniformed workers, uniformed both in the sense of wearing the costume of their franchise but also in the sense of uniformly following the conventions of teenage "beauty"—which was not beauty, but a sublimity of perfect exchangeability, the roller skates themselves

Hypermarket

a gesture, albeit dated, towards capital's lubricity. Every flake or piece of puffed corn belonging to me as good belonged to you—Warhol is the Whitman of the actual: "A Coke is a Coke and no amount of money can get you a better Coke than the one the bum on the corner is drinking. All the Cokes are the same and all the Cokes are good." The same goodness, the good sameness: the energy that coursed through me, undid me, at Hypermart—a store that to the snot-nosed me was what Mont Blanc was to Shelley—I consider that energy integral to poetry. "Money is a kind of poetry," Wallace Stevens said; like money it mediates between the individual and the collective, dissolves the former into the latter or lets the former reform out of the latter only to dissolve again. Do you remember that sense (or have it now) of being a tentative node in a limitless network of goods and flows? Because that's also poetry, albeit in a perverted form, wherein relations between people must appear as things. The affect of abstract exchange, the feeling that everything is fungible—what is its song? The actual song of my early youth might be '80s synthpop, but the impulse that gives rise to it, I maintain, is Poetry.

Or that summer I was at Back to Nature Day Camp at Gage Park and there was a heat wave and the confused teenaged counselors, in order to keep us from sunstroke, took us to see a one-dollar matinee at Gage 4 Theater five days in a row. I remember *Planet of the Apes*—all the younger campers wept with terror. I want only to note that each time the houselights dimmed—these were the first movies I'd ever seen in a theater without the emotional buffer of my family—I felt that other worlds were possible, felt all my senses had been reset and sharpened, that some of them were melding with those of the other kids with their giant Cokes in the dark beside me. This faded quickly as the film progressed and the image of a particular alternative world appeared before us on the screen; there was no trace of it by the time we were rereleased into the preternaturally bright day; but each time the lights went down and the first preview lit up the screen, I felt overwhelmed by an abstract capacity I associate with Poetry. Not the

A Coke is a Coke
is a Coke

The Nature Theater
of Topeka

artwork itself—even when the artwork is great—but the little clearing the theater makes. (A few summers ago I attended an aggressively mediocre opera—not that I know anything about opera—at a gorgeous outdoor theater in Santa Fe, and when my boredom had deepened into something like a trance, I happened to see from our distant seats a single firefly slowly flashing around the orchestra, then floating onto the stage, then drifting back beyond the proscenium: its light appearing here in New Mexico and then three leagues from Seville, here in clock time and there in the continuous present tense of art. Since then I've been attending outdoor theater when I can, less interested in the particular play than in watching, say, a police helicopter over Central Park drift into the air space over the Forest of Arden—while, back in the historical present, I like to imagine, the suspect escapes.)

It is on the one hand a mundane experience and on the other an experience of the structure behind the mundane, patches of unprimed canvas peeking through the real. And—why not speak of it—fucking and getting fucked-up was part of it, is, the way sex and substances can liquefy the particulars of perception into an experience of form. The way a person's stutter can be liquefied by song.

Excerpted from Ben Lerner, *The Hatred of Poetry*, New York: Farrar, Straus and Giroux, 2016. Reprinted with permission from Farrar, Straus and Giroux and the author.

+   Bernd Scherer is Director of the Haus der Kulturen der
Welt (HKW). The philosopher and author of several publications
came to HKW in 2006 after his work as Director of the Goethe-
Institut Mexico. His theoretical work focuses on aesthetics,
philosophy of language, semiotics, and international cultural
exchange. He has curated and co-curated several cultural
and art projects, such as *Agua-Wasser* (2003), *Über Lebens-
kunst* (2010–11), *The Anthropocene Project* (2013–14), *100
Years of Now* (2015–19), and *The New Alphabet* (2019–22).
Since January 2011 he has also been teaching at the Institute
for European Ethnology, Humboldt-Universität zu Berlin.
Amongst many publications, he edited *Die Zeit der Algorithmen*
(2016) and co-edited *Das Anthropozän. Zum Stand der Dinge*
(2015), the four-volume work *Textures of the Anthropocene:
Grain Vapor Ray* (2015), and *Wörterbuch der Gegenwart* (2019).

+   Ann Cotten is an author, translator, and literary theorist living in Vienna and Berlin. She has published numerous volumes of poetry: *Fremdwörterbuchsonette* (2007), *Florida-Räume* (2010), *I, Coleoptile* (2010), *Hauptwerk. Softsoftporn* (2013), and *Lather in Heaven!* (2016); short stories: *Der schaudernde Fächer* (2013) and *Lyophilia* (2019); and epic poetry: *Das Pferd* (2009) and *Verbannt!* (2016), for which she received numerous prizes. In 2018 she was admit- ted to the Akademie der Künste, Berlin. Her translations of Isabel Waidner, Joe Wenderoth, and Mary MacLane were published in 2019, two translations of Rosmarie Waldrop in 2020. She is a Fellow at IFK (Internationales Forschungszentrum Kulturwissenschaften, Kunstuniversität Linz in Vienna), researching the recyclability of humanistic theories with regard to an aesthetics which is comprehensible for machines, too.

+   Yuk Hui currently teaches at the City University of Hong Kong. He has published widely on the philosophy of technology and media in periodicals such as *Research in Phenomenology*; *Metaphilosophy*; *Cahiers Simondon*; *Deleuze Studies*; *Techné*; and *Theory, Culture & Society*. He is co-editor of the anthology *30 Years after Les Immatériaux: Art, Science, Theory* (2015); and author of *On the Existence of Digital Objects* (prefaced by Bernard Stiegler, 2016), *The Question Concerning Technology in China: An Essay in Cosmotechnics* (2017), and *Recursivity and Contingency* (2019). His latest book is *Art and Cosmotechnics* (Fall 2020).

+   Ben Lerner is a poet, novelist, and critic. He is the author of three novels: *Leaving the Atocha Station* (2011), *10:04* (2014), and *The Topeka School* (2019); three books of poetry: *The Lichtenberg Figures* (2004), *Angle of Yaw* (2006), and *Mean Free Path* (2011); and a work of criticism: *The Hatred of Poetry* (2016). He is Distinguished Professor of English at Brooklyn College, City University of New York. His collaboration with Alexander Kluge, *The Snows of Venice / Schnee über Venedig*, was published in German and English by Spector Books in 2018.

+   Kanako Tada is an artist. Her lens is focused to the moment
of genre itself as it becomes the subject matter. She works
with her interests: history of painting, craftsmanship within high-
art, and representations of pattern and materiality. Her works
have been exhibited at *Parallax Trading*, curated by Miwa
Negoro, das weisse haus, Vienna and various exhibitions in
Japan and abroad. Tada is currently on a grant from the Pola Art
Foundation. She holds an MA from Musashino Art University,
Tokyo, and is enrolled in Contextual Painting at the Academy
of Fine Arts, Vienna.

+   Wolfgang Tillmans is an artist. His work combines intimacy
and playfulness with social critique and the questioning of
existing values and hierarchies. He became known in the early
1990s for his pioneering photos of youth and popular culture.
His work has since expanded to include a wide variety of
genres and photographic practices. From the 2000s—with his
Silver, *Lighter*, *Freischwimmer* and *Greifbar* series—he has
been developing new pictorial worlds of abstract photography
that focus on image carriers and exposure processes. In
2000 he was the first photographer and non-UK artist to be
awarded the Turner Prize. Most recently he has exhibited
at Tate Modern in London and the Fondation Beyeler in Basel
(both 2017), the Carré d'Art – Musée d'art contemporain in
Nîmes and the IMMA in Dublin (both 2018), and at WIELS – Centre
for Contemporary Art in Brussels (2020).

Das Neue Alphabet (The New Alphabet) is a publication series by HKW (Haus der Kulturen der Welt).

The series is part of the HKW project *Das Neue Alphabet* (2019–2022), supported by the Federal Government Commissioner for Culture and the Media due to a ruling of the German Bundestag.

Series Editors: Detlef Diederichsen, Anselm Franke,
    Katrin Klingan, Daniel Neugebauer, Bernd Scherer
Project Management: Philipp Albers
Managing Editor: Martin Hager
Copy-Editing: Mandi Gomez, Hannah Sarid de Mowbray
Design Concept: Olaf Nicolai with Malin Gewinner,
    Hannes Drißner

Vol. 1: *The New Alphabet*
Editor: Bernd Scherer
Coordination: Philipp Albers
Contributors: Ann Cotten, Yuk Hui, Ben Lerner, Bernd Scherer,
    Wolfgang Tillmans
Translations: Kevin Kennedy, John Rayner
Graphic Design: Malin Gewinner, Hannes Drißner,
    Markus Dreßen
Type-Setting: Hannah Witte
Fonts: FK Raster (Florian Karsten), Suisse BP Int'l (Ian Party),
    Lyon Text (Kai Bernau)
Image Editing: Scancolor Reprostudio GmbH, Leipzig
Printing and Binding: Gutenberg Beuys Feindruckerei GmbH,
    Langenhagen

Published by:
Spector Books
Harkortstr. 10
01407 Leipzig
www.spectorbooks.com

Distribution:
Germany, Austria: GVA Gemeinsame Verlagsauslieferung
      Göttingen GmbH & Co. KG, www.gva-verlage.de
Switzerland: AVA Verlagsauslieferung AG, www.ava.ch
France, Belgium: Interart Paris, www.interart.fr
UK: Central Books Ltd, www.centralbooks.com
USA, Canada, Central and South America, Africa:
      ARTBOOK | D.A.P. www.artbook.com
Japan: twelvebooks, www.twelve-books.com
South Korea: The Book Society, www.thebooksociety.org
Australia, New Zealand: Perimeter Distribution,
      www.perimeterdistribution.com

Haus der Kulturen der Welt
John-Foster-Dulles-Allee 10
D-10557 Berlin
www.hkw.de

Haus der Kulturen der Welt is a business division of Kultur-
veranstaltungen des Bundes in Berlin GmbH (KBB).

Director: Bernd Scherer
Managing Director: Charlotte Sieben
Chairwoman of the Supervisory Board: Federal
      Government Commissioner for Culture and the Media
      Prof. Monika Grütters MdB

Haus der Kulturen der Welt is supported by

Minister of State
for Culture and the Media

Federal Foreign Office

First Edition
Printed in Germany
ISBN: 978-3-95905-453-9